AERO SERIES VOL. 28

MCDONNELL DOUGLAS
F-15 EAGLE

by

James Perry Stevenson

AERO PUBLISHERS, INC.

329 West Aviation Road, Fallbrook, CA 92028

Library of Congress Card No. 78-17244

Library of Congress Cataloging in Publication Data

Stevenson, James Perry.
  McDonnell Douglas F-15 Eagle.

  (Aero series ; v. 28)
  Includes index.
  1. Eagle (Jet fighter plane)   I.   Title.
UG1242.F5S75   623.74'64   78-17244
ISBN 0-8168-0604-7

TABLE OF CONTENTS

Cover Art Credit: McDonnell Douglas

*To **John Dennison** who made the impossible happen, and **Diane**, of course.*

PREFACE

People pick up a book like this for different reasons. Modellers hope that they will find certain kinds of information for working on their works of art; the aviation buff wants general information; and the aviation historian hopes that he will find some nuggets that will help him further his research.

The length of the *Aero Series* does not lend itself to an exhaustive treatise on the F-15. Furthermore, the F-15 is currently in a dynamic state with new events happening all the time. An example is the recent vote to sell F-15s to Saudi Arabia.

In an attempt to make this book more flexible, and work as a tool for modeller, buff, and particularly the aviation historian, I'm going to follow this brief preface with a short annotated bibliography which will spring the reader into many of the areas I've been, and became frustrated because of not being able to include all of the good information in those sources. Hopefully, you will get more out of this book because of this short bibliography.

ANNOTATED BIBLIOGRAPHY

Aviation Week & Space Technology, McGraw-Hill, New York.

There are so many excellent articles on the F-15, that one must look them up. There is no space here to list them all. Published weekly, this magazine covers the mundane F-15 events, but includes many indepth articles.

Drendel, L. and Don Carson. *F-15 Eagle in Action.* Warren, Michigan: Squadron/Signal Publication, 1976.

Only other English language book on the F-15 at this time. Not much text, but some good line illustrations on details of the F-15.

English, Richard D. "F-14 vs. F-15N: Focus of the Tactical Airpower Controversy." Unpublished paper, Washington University, St. Louis, Missouri, n.d.

A "must" paper for anyone interested in the political decisions surrounding the F-14/F-15 controversy. The paper is unpublished.

"F-15 Eagle." *Flight International*, May 1, 1975.

An excellent overview of the F-15. This article is a classic reading for an F-15 overview, and is the source of the cutaway drawing found on pp. 42-43 of this book.

Eagle Owner's Manual: Your Introduction to the McDonnell F-15, (P.S. 872, Nov. 1974) St. Louis: McDonnell Aircraft Company.

This is a small booklet, complete with a plastic key for the prospective new F-15 owner. Each of the systems is explained by the various test pilots in words anyone can understand.

"F-15 rolls out at St. Louis." *Flight International*, July 6, 1972.

Another good article by *Flight International* describing some of the early history of the F-15, and events that led up to the roll-out.

Geddes, J. Phillip. "High performance and the F-15." *Interavia Review,* February 1975.

Another overview of the F-15 with charts and graphs on its performance.

Koku Fan

This Japanese monthly has many pictures of past and current F-15 paint schemes. It also has good information on the plane itself; unfortunately it is written in Japanese. *Koku Fan* also publishes monthly issues on particular aircraft. The F-15 has also been made a subject of one of these issues.

Levin, Stuart M. "F-15: The Teething of a Dogfighter." *Space/ Aeronautics*, December, 1969, pp. 36-47.

> You won't find this magazine on the current list because it has gone out of business. However, it is one of the best sources for history of military aircraft during the 1960s.

McDonnell Douglas Corporation. *F-15 Aircraft General Orientation Course.* (F-15-092-118) St. Louis, Missouri: McDonnell Aircraft Co., May 1974.

> This is a mimeograph tome written by McAir for a general orientation to the aircraft.

McInerney, Thomas G. "The United States Air Force's Management System for the F-15 Air Superiority Fighter." M.S. dissertation, National War College, 1973.

> While the title may discourage you—if you think that this is just a paper on management—it is an excellent overview of the F-15 from the historical point of view. It also contains an excellent bibliography.

McDonnell Douglas Corporation, *Product Support Digest.*

> This is a publication put out by the Product Support arm of McDonnell Douglas Corporation. It comes out quarterly, and has articles on the aircraft that McAir is required to support. This is a "must" source for the serious student.

Schemmer, Benjamin F. "The Eagle is Not a Turkey or a Dove." Armed Forces Journal Internation, March 1975.

> A good overview of the F-15 from the air-to-air point of view. Has some performance data comparisons.

Stevenson, James Perry. *Grumman F-14 Tomcat.* Fallbrook, California: Aero Publishers 1975.

> This might be helpful because there is data on the aerodynamics of fighter aircraft, in general, which can be applied to an understanding of the F-15.

Stevenson, James Perry. "F-14 Versus F-15 Flyoffs: Who Would the Real Winner Be?" *Armed Forces Journal International*, June 1975 pp. 40-43.

> This article makes the point of the importance of pilot training— particularly why the F-14 should be allowed to fly against the F-15.

"USAF F-15 Eagle: The Jet Age." Scale Models, Feb. 1975 pp. 65-70.

> An overview of the F-15 models available in 1/72 scale up to the date of the article.

White, William D., *U.S. Tactical Air Power: Missions, Forces, and Costs,* Washington, D.C.: Brookings Institution 1974.

> This is a small 121 page paperback that has data on all the latest military fighters, along with some attack and Russian aircraft.

ACKNOWLEDGEMENTS

This book has been in the making for over four years. In that time I've had the pleasure of corresponding with many tremendous people. Taking time to thank them for the first time or once again on this page is one of the more pleasurable jobs associated with writing this book.

Compiling this list is done mainly from reviewing my files of letters to make sure I've included everyone's name. However, there have been a few folks who have been of great assistance that I've not written to or they to me. I've met them through my travels and all our conversations have been oral. To acknowledge them I've scanned the memory core of my mind. Unfortunately, I fear some will be left out of this acknowledgement due to my own lapse of memory. To you who should be here—and are forgotten—to you my sincerest apologies. I thank you again.

These names, then, are by default, a partial listing of some great folks, and to . . .

Liz Scott
Barb Philipps
John E. Severance
Ben Goldman
Don Malvern
Lee Humiston
Lt. Col. Tim O'Keefe USAF
Capt. Rick P. Ducharme USAF
Capt. Jerry L. Hanchey USAF
Major James C. Postgate USAF
Major Allan V. Cummings USAF
Major Richard E. Stevenson USAF
Lt. Col. Eitan Ben Eliyahu IAF
Major Jeff Cliver USAF
Darrell Gary
Dr. Rich Oberle
The Topgun Staff
Ted Bear
Richard P. Lutz
Donald S. McGarry
Paul Sewell
Don Logan
Phil Houston
Chet Brawn
Paul Homsher
Irv Burrows
Shirley J. Bach
Robert "Beaver" Blake
Jim Kelly
Gen. Robert J. Dixon USAF
Col. R. R. Moore USAF
Col. Don Byrnes USAF
Major Gen. Robert C. Mathis USAF
Roger Mathews
Herman Hamm
Richard Noyes
Robert Eberhard
William Murden
Don Adams
Ed Furtek
McDonnell Flight Test

Henry Overal
C. E. "Bud" Anderson
Col. Wendell Shawler USAF
Lt. Col. Mac MacFarland USAF
Major J. Saravo USAF
Lt. Col. Roger Smith USAF
Major Walt Vbralic USAF
John H. Bickers
R. J. Davis
Capt. John V. Alexander USAF
Capt. Herbert G. Baker USAF
Capt. Spencer W. Wilkerson USAF
Sharon Briggs
Glenn H. Briggs
Keith Ferris
Keith Wallis
Ben Park
Roy Wendell
Mike Heenan
George Graff
Col. Jack Petry USAF
Capt. Don G. Kline USAF
Major Tom C. Skanchy USAF
Major Dennis R. Mangum USAF
Capt. Victor S. Natiello USAF
Col. John F. O'Donnell USAF
Capt. Gerald B. Fleming USAF
Bill Brinks
Major Gerald F. Broening USAF
John J. McGrath
Dennis Jenkins
Mick Roth
Jim Rotramel
Bob Lawson
Lloyd S. Jones
Pete Garrison
Denver D. Clark
Carl D. Counts
Toby Hughes
Michael France

. . . I thank you again.

When the North American F-86 *Sabre* took off for the first time in May, 1948, it looked like the harbinger of jet fighter aircraft. The F-86 was sleek, with the full vision cockpit that became the familiar sight on its predecessor, the P-51 *Mustang*. In fact, the *Sabre* seemed to be a culmination of all that was learned in World War II fighter tactics, but with the addition of a jet engine. The wing loading—critically important for a maneuverable dogfighter—stayed relatively low, around 56 pounds per square foot at combat gross weight, which was only six pounds more than the P-51D's. All this was done in keeping with the design concept of the F-86—air superiority.

History of

The list of Air Force jet fighters between the F-86 *Sabre* and the first flight of the F-15 *Eagle* is impressively devoid of any whose designed mission was air superiority. The F-89, F-94, and the century series fighters were either interceptor or fighter-bomber aircraft. The F-4 *Phantom*, which was a Navy developed aircraft, originally conceived as an attack aircraft (AH-1), was converted to an interceptor during design, but fortunately, had enough characteristics of an air superiority dogfight-capable aircraft to hold its own in the Viet Nam war, as a fighter and as a bomber.

The shift away from the World War I, World War II, and Korean concept of what it takes to dominate the aerial battleground resulted from the development of beyond visual range missiles. Although the first interceptors were designed to fly until they acquired visual contact, and then shoot down the incoming

Development

bombers with rockets, the advancement of technology allowed fighter aircraft to fire missiles at targets seen only on their radar screens.

The first practical application of this beyond visual range method of maintaining air supremacy began during the beginning of the Viet Nam war. The problems were immediate. No longer did the pilot have a clean radar scope with only "bad" guys on it as the interceptors did in the exercises of the late 1950s and early 1960s. Now he had everybody on his radar scope. There were two more problems that kept the pilot from using his beyond visual range *Sparrow* missile. The first was his Identification Friend or Foe (IFF) which was supposed to designate whether the target was an enemy or not. The second was the politics of the war itself. The IFF often malfunctioned so that on more than one occasion Americans shot down fellow pilots in the early part of the war. Once the pilots received an IFF system that worked properly, they weren't allowed to use it. The politics of the war prevented American pilots from taking advantage of their favorable arenas, which necessarily put them into the enemy's arena. These restraints required that an aircraft designed as an interceptor, with a pilot trained for an interceptor mission, forget that mission and gear up for a dogfight since visual acquisition was one of the rules of engagement.

Getting into a dogfight with the MiG-17s and MiG-21, the only probable outcome of visually identifying another aircraft, was risky business. The kill-loss ratio for the U.S. Air Force during the Viet Nam war was slightly over 2:1. Compare this ratio to the better than 10:1 kill-loss ratio the U.S. Air Force had in Korea against some of the same type aircraft—MiG-15s (essentially a detuned MiG-17)—and the idea that the military thinking should come full circle becomes obvious.

Sixty years of fighter aviation are parked next to each other at Robbins AFB. The SPAD with the markings of the 94th Aero Squadron which is one of the squadrons in the 1st Tactical Fighter Wing.

(McDonnell Douglas)

During the pre-production Category I test phase, the F-15 experienced an undesirable buffet at certain points in the flight envelope. These wing fences were an attempt to solve that problem. The problem was concurrently eliminated when the wing tips were raked 4 square feet to eliminate a large wing bending moment. *(McDonnell Douglas)*

In spite of the long period of interceptor-type fighters, the Air Force had a contingent within it that was pushing for the air superiority type fighter that was exemplified by the P-51 and F-86. In the early 1960s the need for a study started expressing itself throughout the fighter community in the Air Force. These studies had the generic name of Fighter Experimental (FX).

In April 1965, the original FX studies began. In October of that same year, the Air Force asked for funding to begin full scale studies, only to follow up this request for funding with Request for Proposals (RFP) for a Tactical Support Aircraft in December 1965. McDonnell Aircraft Company, the eventual winner of the FX program, was one of the five losers in the four-month Concept Formulation Study. The Study's went to North American Rockwell, Lockheed Aircraft, and Boeing, in March 1966. McDonnell did its own in-house FX investigations from March to December 1966.

The Air Force was not completely satisfied with all of the designs that were generated out of the first Concept Formulation Study, and as a result, picked none. The primary reasons were the aerodynamic configuration and the by-pass ratio of the engine.

From the middle of 1966 to the fall of 1967 there was no overt activity on the FX. In the background, however, the Air Force was maintaining its own Concept Formulation Study team which lasted approximately two years—from the fall of 1966 to the fall of 1968.

There was some excitement during the period from middle of 1966 to the fall of 1967: the TFX was creating problems for the Department of Defense; the Russians had the now famous Domodadovo Air Show in July 1967. At the Domodadovo Air Show the Russians introduced 12 new aircraft and several new versions of older aircraft. The Air Force intelligence community was quick to respond to this new input and as a result, in August 1967, the Air Force issued a second RFP for a Concept Formulation Study, only this time the name "Tactical Support Aircraft" was gone, and instead the word Fighter was substituted. McDonnell Aircraft Company along with General Dynamics were awarded this second six-month Concept Formulation Study.

The Air Force gave loose objectives. For example, the fighter could be in the 1.5 to 3.0 Mach range. In the background, however, the Aeronautical Systems Division at Wright-Patterson AFB was defining what could be done while at the Air Staff level Major John Boyd with the assistance of Mr. Tom Christie at Eglin AFB, and Everest Riccioni were saying what should be done.

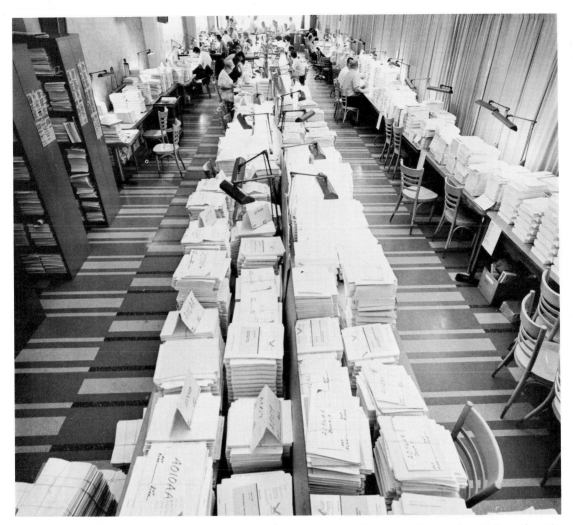

This is the McDonnell Aircraft Co. answer to the Request for Proposal. It's hard to believe that six months later in December 1969 the Air Force could have finished reading the presentation, much less decided the winner. *(McDonnell Douglas)*

The General Dynamics FX study group recommended both a fixed wing and a variable geometry FX, while the McDonnell Aircraft Company group recommended fixed wing, two engines and a single crew. This second Concept Formulation Study ran through May 1968. In September, the Deputy Secretary of Defense approved the FX Concept Development paper.

That same month, the Air Force released an RFP for Contract Definition to the Aerospace industry. The Request for Proposal was sent to McDonnell Douglas, North American, Grumman, General Dynamics, Lockheed, LTV, Fairchild Hiller and Boeing. Three months later, the Air Force awarded contracts to McDonnell Douglas, North American and Fairchild Hiller for Contract Definition. Interestingly enough, during this period between RFP and Contract

Definition award, on October 10th, the participants were told to consider the Navy in their design.

These three companies, then, started off the 1969 New Year with the hope of winning the fighter-aviation contract of the century. From January through June of that year these aerospace titans applied their individual collective management and engineering knowledge, with the one goal: win the F-15 development and production contract, a contract with the potential worth of $7.3 billion. At the end of this six-month period the Air Force took over. From July 1969 until December 1969, the Air Force at the Aeronautical Systems Division (ASD) evaluated the three proposals. On December 23, at 3:30 p.m.EST 1969, McDonnell Douglas was announced as the winner of the prime contract on the F-15.

THE THREAT

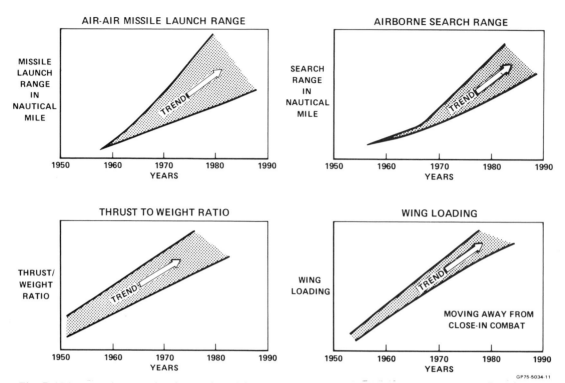

The F-15 has set the pace for threat aircraft in all these areas but one — wing loading. The F-15 has very low wing loading, while maintaining its ability to dash at interceptor-like speeds. (McDonnell Douglas)

No aircraft is designed in a vacuum; they are always designed to answer a known or postulated threat. The particular threat that the F-15 was designed to overcome, however, was a trend more than a specific aircraft. The airshow at Domodadovo in July of 1967 had put a jolt into the intelligence community. This information quickly entered the system and the Air Force sent it out to the designers at the McDonnell Aircraft Company division of McDonnell Douglas Corporation and to the other FX contenders.

The Russians had for a long time built aircraft whose purpose was point defense. These aircraft had a limited range, but were small enough that they could be scattered all over the homeland to defend against a potential threat. As the threat to the Russians changed, so did *their* design philosophy, and it is over this trend that the F-15 designers were scratching their heads. However, they were working on an answer that would be even better.

The Russian trend over the last twenty years has been an increase in air-to-air missile launch range, radar search range, thrust-to-weight ratio, and higher wing loading. To this trend

there has been an increase in the percentage of beyond-visual-range type fighters, with a corresponding decrease in the percentage of clear air mass fighters, which the MiG-17, -19, and -21 exemplify. By matching our aircraft design with the Russians, we could believe that the interceptor-type aircraft that the F-4 *Phantom* represents is the proper direction toward which to design our aircraft (even though the F-4 had relatively low wing loading for an interceptor). Unfortunately, this trend, e.g., high thrust to weight with high wing loading does not help in a dogfight. High thrust to weight is a desirable commodity because the more thrust from the engines, the more velocity or more energy for creating maneuvers. High wing loading, on the other hand, decreases maneuvering performance. The trend by the Russians and by the Air Force (and for that matter the Navy since the F-4 *Phantom* was developed by the Navy) has been to develop a plane that could dash out at top speeds to intercept the incoming threat.

Along with this trend, however, there has been an increasing number of versions of the MiG-21, which although it has interceptor-like speed, but with no complimentary armament,

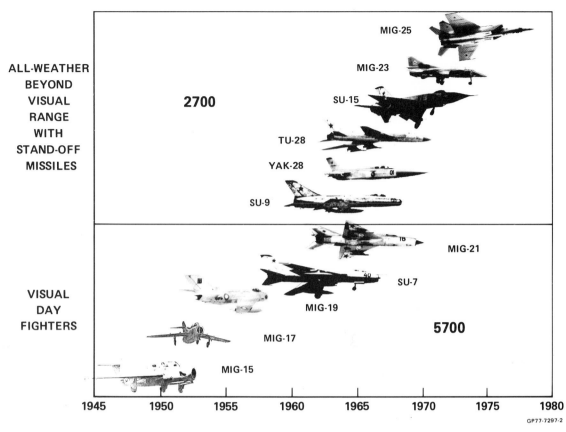

ALL-WEATHER BEYOND VISUAL RANGE WITH STAND-OFF MISSILES

2700

MIG-25
MIG-23
SU-15
TU-28
YAK-28
SU-9

VISUAL DAY FIGHTERS

MIG-21
SU-7
MIG-19
5700
MIG-17
MIG-15

1945   1950   1955   1960   1965   1970   1975   1980

GP77-7297-2

This chart shows the evolution of the trend in Russian fighter philosophy. As the years increase, so does the "beyond visual range" radar capability and the corresponding capability of the missiles carried. Even the heretofore strictly visual MiG-21 is being modified for the "beyond visual range" mission.

(McDonnell Douglas)

also has the ability to get into a scrap and do an honest job of dogfighting. With this capability is the added threat of the MiG-21 having been distributed to countries around the world in large numbers.

The Russians, then, have been developing interceptor fighters, at the same time perfecting a dogfighter that was proving itself very capable in the Viet Nam war. In fact, in early 1968, the North Vietnamese were getting a better kill-loss ratio than American pilots. In spite of these good dogfighting characteristics, the MiG-21 has limited capability beyond visual range, and therefore, since the trend of air-to-air missile launch range is increasing, it would not be the fighter to completely emulate. What would seem to be the ideal combination, would be a fighter that had dogfighting capabilities and yet retain the beyond visual range and dash speed capabilities of an interceptor. In short, from an aerodynamic point of view, what was needed is a low wing loading along with high thrust to

weight, and from an avionic point of view, a capable interceptor-type beyond visual range weapons system.

Wing loading, (the weight of the aircraft, divided by the area of the lifting surface), is a critical component in a turning dogfight. Wing loading has been varied by aeronautical engineers for years depending on what mission was planned for the aircraft. Give a wing more area, and its increase in lifting ability would aerodynamically follow. One characteristic that would not follow, though, and that was a corresponding increase in thrust to overcome the parasite drag that an increase in lifting area would create at higher speeds. It is precisely this increase in drag that forced designers to make smaller and smaller wings to get more and more speed out of the engines' available thrust. On the other hand, the designers were not tasked with designing an air combat maneuvering (ACM)-type fighter so they did not explore that arena.

CONFIGURATION EVOLUTION

STUDIES AND TESTS

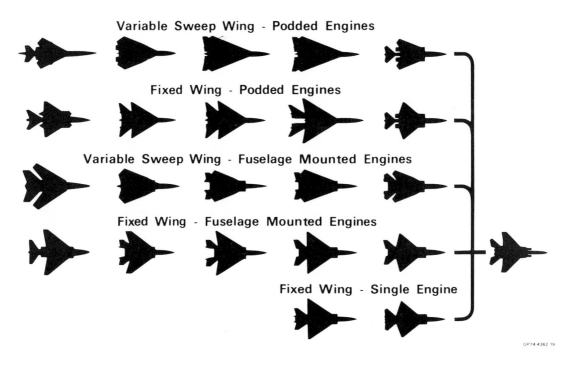

Compare these planforms of the various artist drawings on pages 20-21. Notice the design second from the left in the third row from the top. It looks similar to the F-14A Tomcat in full wing sweep.

(McDonnell Douglas)

With the Request for Proposal which the Air Force let in September 1968, McDonnell Douglas, as did the other companies, had a new set of problems which included exploring the recently heretofore unexplored air combat maneuvering arena. Since the Request for Proposal is the guiding light for the aerospace industry to follow (although in many cases, the industry is asked to tell the services what would be reasonable to ask), the RFP summary shows what the Air Force was looking for:

(a) A wing optimized for high load factor and buffet-free performance at 0.9 Mach at 30,000 feet (9,100M).

(b) High thrust-to-weight ratio to achieve very high energy maneuverability throughout the flight envelope when combined with the wing criteria noted in (a) above.

(c) Global ferry range capability with or without inflight refueling.

(d) One-man operation of the weapon system for all missions.

(e) A realistic air-to-air fighter fatigue spectrum with a life of 4000 hours and a scatter factor of 4. This required testing to

16,000 hours (without structural failure).

(f) Advanced cockpit layout, displays, and controls which would allow heads-up operation during close-in combat.

(g) A reduction in Maintenance Man Hours per Flight Hour (MMH/FH) to typical W.W. II fighter levels of 11.3 MMH/FH.

(h) A significant increase in avionic and airframe subsystem component Mean Time Between Failures (MTBF) in order to achieve the 11.3 MMH/FH requirement.

(i) 360° cockpit visibility.

(j) Self-contained engine starting without use of ground support equipment.

(k) Highly survivable structure, fuel, hydraulic, flight control, and electrical subsystems in a combat environment for safe return to base.

(l) A maximum Air Superiority mission gross weight in the 40,000 pound (18,100 Kg.) class.

(m) Low development risk components and subsystems which had been proven in prototype, pre-production, or production-type components. For example, both the

14

WING DEVELOPMENT

107 WINGS WIND TUNNEL TESTED
800 VARIATIONS ANALYZED

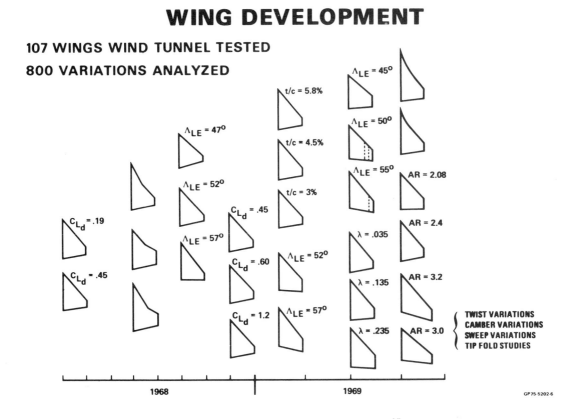

Some of the 107 wings that were wind tunnel tested to arrive at the final solution for the F-15.

(McDonnell Douglas)

engines and radar were being developed and tested on Air Force funded competitive prototype development test programs along with the airframe study and proposal effort.

(n) Mach 2.5 maximum capability at altitude.

(o) Long-range Pulse Doppler radar with look-down capability.

The F-15 parameters essentially defined, the trade-off studies began. McDonnell Douglas was nervous because it had never won a paper airplane contest. On the other hand, McAir (as it is called in the industry) had never lost under the older X-prototype concept. McDonnell Douglas had the feeling that if the services could see their product, then that would be what would sell airplanes. McDonnell Douglas had lost some significant airplanes on paper: F-111 and the VFX. They were really trying with the VFX.

McDonnell Douglas was fortunate that it had so much experience with the U.S. Navy in designing aircraft to come aboard aircraft carriers. The Air Force could pave the world in order to give its steamlined interceptors enough runway to land on; not so the Navy. Coming

down the final approach to a carrier created a requirement that the aircraft be able to fly at slow speeds and high angles of attack. This had never been an Air Force requirement, but the Air Force benefited from McAir's experience in this area. This ability to fly at high angles of attack is required in an air combat maneuvering aircraft.

The trade-off studies on the wing were designed around a lift over drag (L/D) maximized for fighting, not cruising. There was a dearth of data in that area. It had been years since wind tunnels had been looking in the air combat maneuvering area so when McDonnell Douglas turned to NASA, usually a good source for experimental data, they were surprised to find NASA dormant. McAir tooled up. Three wind tunnels were kept busy almost around the clock for nearly a year. The ultimate wing was selected from some 800 analyzed configurations, with 107 wings wind tunnel tested. The total number of wind tunnel hours on the F-4 *Phantom* was 4287, to first flight, while the F-15 required 22,188, five times the testing required on the *Phantom*.

In pursuing the F-X, McDonnell Douglas ex-

15

perimented with 25,000 pound aircraft up to 100,000 pound aircraft. They experimented with 68 different point designs. One of the internal design groups at McDonnell Douglas was tasked with taking all the characteristics that make up a good fighter and merging with these the structure cost and a flexible "rubber" engine, and dumping them into a computer to do trade studies. One of the interesting observations of these studies that CADE (Computer Aided Design and Evaluation) made showed that if you continue to spend money, the customer can continue to get specific excess power, which is the power the fighter has left to climb or turn when pulling *g*s.

The RFP called for a 40,000 pound airplane. The trade-off studies narrowed the final concept of the F-15. Engineers traded 6.5 *g* at 60% fuel requirement against 8 *g*s with 100% fuel requirement. This trade gave a 38,000 and 41,500

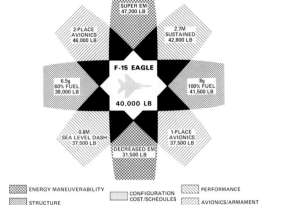

This "snowflake" diagram shows the trade-off to arrive at a 40,000 pound design.
(McDonnell Douglas)

COMPUTER AIDED DESIGN EVALUATION PROGRAM

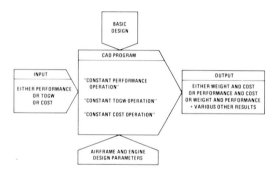

With a Computer Aided Design Evaluation (CADE) program, the McAir engineers were able to take the various input and iterate them with gross weight, cost, engines available, and design limitation to develop comparison trade-off. The chart below shows takeoff gross weight compared with mission radius. Imposed on this is combat time and constant energy-maneuverability.
(McDonnell Douglas)

F-15 CADE STUDIES
TAKEOFF GROSS WEIGHT vs MISSION RADIUS

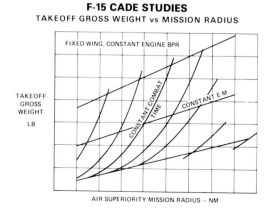

pound airplane respectively. Super energy maneuverability required a 47,200 pound F-15 while a decreased energy maneuverability F-15 would weigh in at 31,500. The five different suits of avionics—two man all-weather (similar to the A-6E) versus one man clear air mass stretched the weight between 46,000 and 37,500 pounds. At this same light weight, the F-15 could have a sea level dash of 0.8 Mach while at 42,800 it could sustain 2.7 Mach. From all of these trades, the F-15 fell out with a weight of about 40,000 pounds.

In designing fighter aircraft there is always a monetary limitation placed upon the program. This has always been a reality, but in the current times of detente and post-war cutbacks, the emphasis on fiscal limitation is even greater. Given an amount of money, then the designers are tasked not only with a given aircraft to design, but more fundamentally they have to analyze the threat and the threat's estimated numbers. To minimize the amount of money spent on a given program, then, the designers have to weight the scales between more numbers and less capabilities, or more capabilities and less numbers.

The process by which McDonnell Douglas engineers go through involves the analysis of the threat both ground and air weapons and electronics, and then the development of a matrix which will list all the possible requirements to counter the threat. With this information, they then build a baseline aircraft that can grow both dimensionally and geometrically. This baseline design is then subjected to McAir's multi-technology aircraft sizing to fill the matrix in order to determine the size and

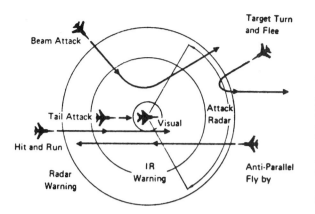

Engagement starting condition.
(McDonnell Douglas)

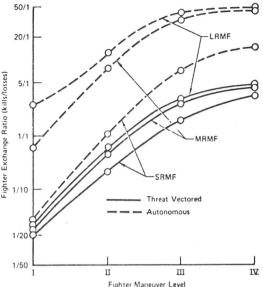

The Computer Aided Design Evaluation (CADE) compares short, medium, and long range missile fighters against the MiG-21-type day fighter showing the kill-loss ratio increasing as the computer fighter maneuverability increases.
(McDonnell Douglas)

geometrical shape the answer to the threat should take. These various configurations are then flown in the simulator against a computerized threat. As a result of the simulation the optimum aircraft is selected.

For the sake of discussion, the threat force structure is made up of three classes of aircraft. The dayfighter is a close-in dueling aircraft with short range missiles. It is sometimes referred to as a short range missile fighter (SRMF). The fighter-interceptor has better maneuverability than the dayfighter with the addition of stand-off missile capability. This class is often referred to as an intermediate missile range fighter (IRMF). The high-altitude threat has long range lookdown and shoot-down missile capability, with a reduced maneuvering capability from either of the other two aircraft classes. It is often referred to as a long range missile fighter (LRMF). The short range missile is of the *Sidewinder* class, the medium range missile is of the advanced *Sparrow* class, and the long range missile is of the *Phoenix* class. In addition to the three suits of avionic and missile systems (the avionic systems correspond with the capability of the missiles) the tentative fighter matrix shows four levels of maneuverability. Level 1 is inferior to the dayfighter threat, level 2 is equal to the dayfighter threat, level 3 is equal to fighter-interceptor threat, and level 4 is superior to fighter-interceptor threat. The high altitude fighter's maneuverability is not at issue because maneuverability is not its style.

All of the possible fighter designs are required to fly the same mission, so in the development of the optimum answer to the threat, the McAir engineers require all the matrix aircraft to fly the same mission profile.

Different aircraft will do better in different parts of the flight envelope. These conflicting size requirements are a function of four major aerodynamic functions. The maximum Mach number would drive the design toward high wing loading, as would acceleration. Maneuverability, with its corresponding specific excess power (P_s) drives the design toward low wing loading and low induced drag wing design. The fourth factor, the maximum load factor, usually drives the design toward lower wing loading and affects the size of the empennage for desired flight control and stability.

The Computer Aided Design Evaluation (CADE) is a large software program that lets the engineers build a baseline aircaft, and then vary it to change it with the threat matrix. CADE can make changes with the engine, aircraft design, mission description, performance requirements, and finally change or alter the avionics and missiles carried. To all these factors, the CADE program can impose the unit life cycle costs of the various classes of fighters—day, interceptor, or high altitude—and maneuvering level.

To determine the fighter effectiveness, the fighter is put in simulated engagement starting conditions, with the threat having ground controllers in one scenario, and no vectoring in the other. The threat aircraft is put in engagement positions from the beam, tail, and engages in tactics like hit and run, turn and flee, and anti-parallel fly by. In a threat vectored environment, the kill-loss ratio is poor for the fighter until it is given either a medium range missile or advanced to the third or fourth maneuvering level.

Finally, the fighter designed in the McAir computer is cast against the threat in numbers. The threat is given a total of 1,000 aircraft broken up into three force mixes. This mix is a transition from a majority of dayfighters to an increase of the more sophisticated fighter-interceptor. This model is, of course, significant because of the current Russian trend. The computer then determines the number of fighter aircraft necessary to defeat the threat aircraft by force mix. The computer gives the numbers necessary by each of the three classes— SRMF, MRMF, and LRMF—and by maneuvering level. The optimum design is then influenced by the force structure of the estimated threat.

One of the considerations in the design stage was whether to make the F-15 *Eagle* a one or two man aircraft. Lt. General John Burns, then Col. Burns with the 8th Tactical Fighter Wing (TFW) was influential in driving the Air Force to the one man concept. The Air Force procedure in Viet Nam was to have the Ground Control Intercept personnel tell the pilot that a bogey had popped up on his tail and closing fast. This usually required the pilot to pull a 180 degree turn. The resulting fast rate of closure and poor crew coordination due to high speed of closure caused the Air force to get very few good *Sparrow* missile shots off. In fact they had 50 misses in the beginning of the war, which was a major factor leading up to Col. Burns decision to recommend the one man mission. The Air Force did not have the dedicated back seat missile operators that the Navy had. Usually they were pilots who were putting in their time until they could get into the front seat. A control stick in the back seat of the Air Force F-4s was one of the distinguishing features between the Air Force F-4s and the Navy's. Those Air Force back seaters who were not pilots, but dedicated Weapon System Officer (WSO) did not regularly fly with the same pilot, which was the Navy policy, so this, too, lent to the crew coordination problem. The Air Force experience told them that with the automation built into the F-15, it will only take one man.

As a result of Deputy Secretary of Defense Nitze encouraging the aerospace manufac-turers that they should include the possibility of a Navyized version of the F-15, McDonnell Douglas said that their model 199-1B (proposed F-15A) was adaptable to carrier service due to excellent visibility and thrust to weight. McAir told the Air Force that the F-15A would be suitable to operate off carriers of the CVA-19 class or larger and that the only modifications that would have to be made would be landing gear for strength catapult tow, wing fold for carrier storage, and arresting hook strength for carrier landings.

On July 8, 1971, the Navy sought data on the F-15 as a potential fighter. The Secretary of Defense asked the Navy to investigate via the Systems Program Office (SPO) the possibility of an F-15N. McAir designed a minimum modification which increased the weight approximately 2300 pounds for carrier suitability. The F-15N then became a subject of Navy Fighter Study Group III. The Navy disregarded McAir's data and did their own study in which they increased the weight, and Phoenixed it. This increased the weight and drag so much for the *Phoenix* that performance went down and cost went up to where it was unacceptable.

In another investigation testimony on 30 March 1973 before the Senate Armed Services Committee's *ad hoc* Tactical Air Power subcommittee started new discussions on the possibility of the F-15 being modified for the Navy mission. At this time the Navy's F-14 program was attracting pressure, and as a result, Deputy Secretary of Defense Packard wanted to look at the alternatives to the Navy mission with lower cost F-14s, F-15Ns, and improved F-4s. Deputy Secretary of Defense Clements attempted to obtain funding for the F-14—F-15 flyoff. These discussions, along with other driving forces led up to the forming of Navy Fighter Study IV in which these alternatives were discussed. Out of this study group fell the Naval Air Combat Fighter (NACF) formerly known as VFAX, and ultimately known as the F-18 *Hornet*.

Management is one of the least talked about aspects of new fighter aircraft development outside the aerospace industry. Management, next to the airplane itself, is like comparing the football tackle to the quarterback: One gets all the recognition but the other is what makes it happen. The management of the F-15 has been as impressive as the airplane, and in fact, the airplane's impressiveness is a direct reflection of the F-15 management.

The Air Force's last few airplanes have been

F-15 (N-PHX)
GENERAL ARRANGEMENT

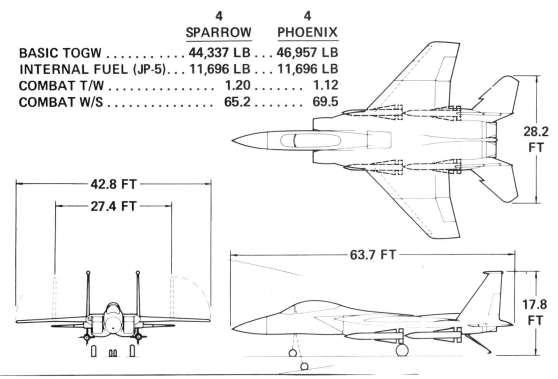

	4 SPARROW	4 PHOENIX
BASIC TOGW	44,337 LB	46,957 LB
INTERNAL FUEL (JP-5)	11,696 LB	11,696 LB
COMBAT T/W	1.20	1.12
COMBAT W/S	65.2	69.5

42.8 FT

27.4 FT

28.2 FT

63.7 FT

17.8 FT

F-15 vs F-14

		F-14A	F-15A
TOGW	lb	56,400	40,000
INT. FUEL	lb	16,440	11,100
T/W (TAKEOFF)		.72	1.2
W/S (TAKEOFF)	lb/ft^2	100	66

14 JANUARY 1971
GP9595 26

19

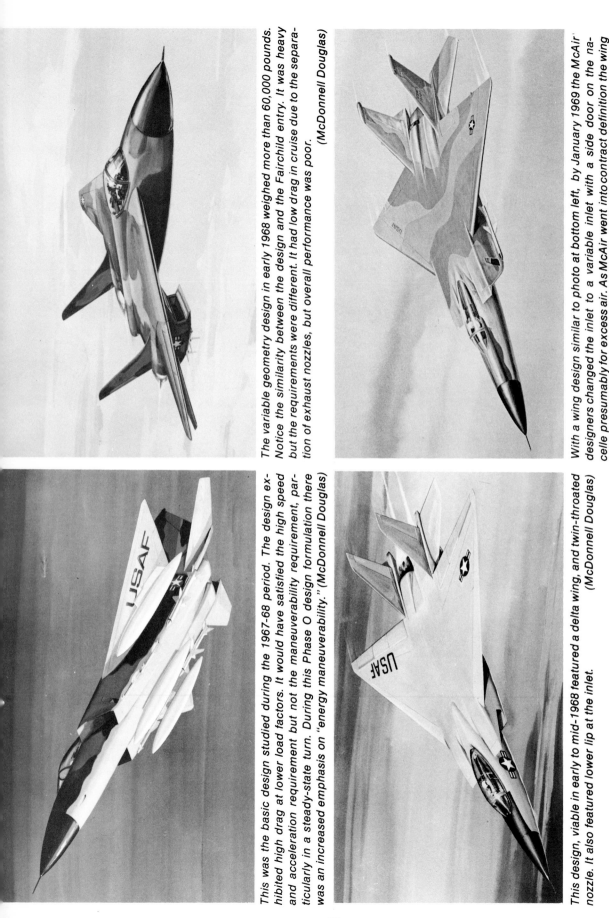

This was the basic design studied during the 1967-68 period. The design exhibited high drag at lower load factors. It would have satisfied the high speed and acceleration requirement but not the maneuverability requirement, particularly in a steady-state turn. During this Phase O design formulation there was an increased emphasis on "energy maneuverability." (McDonnell Douglas)

The variable geometry design in early 1968 weighed more than 60,000 pounds. Notice the similarity between the design and the Fairchild entry. It was heavy but the requirements were different. It had low drag in cruise due to the separation of exhaust nozzles, but overall performance was poor. (McDonnell Douglas)

This design, viable in early to mid-1968 featured a delta wing, and twin-throated nozzle. It also featured lower lip at the inlet. (McDonnell Douglas)

With a wing design similar to photo at bottom left, by January 1969 the McAir designers changed the inlet to a variable inlet with a side door on the nacelle presumably for excess air. As McAir went into contract definition the wing was optionized with a variable camber leading edge. (McDonald Douglas)

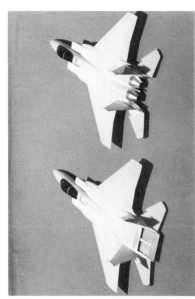

The Fairchild entry into the F-X competition is shown in this artist's rendering. The right and left engine nacelles were interchangeable. The distance between engines also minimized the possibility of one hit knocking out both engines. (Dennis Jenkins Collection)

The rocker-ramp outlet (above left) was designed to operate as a thrust reverser. The trailing edge separated to form a "V" when observed from the side. The Air Force rejected the design because they felt the more conventional design (above right) was less likely to create problems. (NASA)

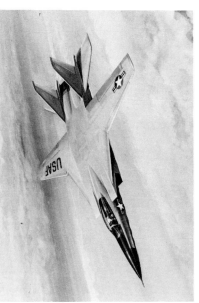

Another variable sweep design with the rocker-ramp two-dimensional exhaust. Notice also the lower lip at the engine inlet. This design, like all variable geometry proposals, was too heavy.
(McDonnell Douglas)

The North American Rockwell entry into the F-X competition with the blended wing has a similar appearance to the YF-16 which evolved several years later.
(Lloyd S. Jones Collection)

This is the F-15 design submitted along with the Fairchild and the North American Rockwell entry for the F-X competition. The shape of the nose was done to improve inlet characteristics for yaw conditions at high angles of attack. (The new nose now on the F-15 is simpler to build, and improves the radar. Notice how the cockpit has been raised.
(McDonnell Douglas)

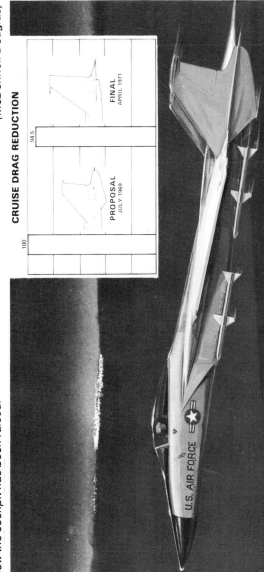

CRUISE DRAG REDUCTION

PROPOSAL JULY 1969

FINAL APRIL 1971

Navy managed projects. The F-4 *Phantom* was originally designed as the AH-1 before the numbering system changed under Secretary of Defense McNamara. Later the mission of the *Phantom* was changed from an attack aircraft to an interceptor. The F-4 program was so successful that the Air Force bought F-4 *Phantoms* and in far greater numbers than the Navy. The Air Force also bought the A-7 which was another Navy managed program. It is little wonder that the Air Force was anxious to have management responsibility for their own air superiority fighter. They had another reason for wanting control of their own program: to redeem themselves from the stigma of the F-111 and the C-5A management fiasco.

The management responsibility on the F-15 has been a joint Air Force-McDonnell Douglas effort, with the Air Force having final responsibility. In this day of operating in the fish-bowl arena, with Congress and the rest of the world watching, the F-15 program, headed by then Col. Benjamin Bellis, did a remarkable job of taking the F-15 from concept through the major portion of the pre-production aircraft. General Bellis came aboard July 1969 from the SR-71 program. One of the major reasons that General Bellis and the F-15 were able to succeed was their anticipation of problem areas. General Bellis through his Information Officer gave complete and indepth briefings rather than risk misinformation to Congress and the public. Many military people minimize the value of public relations, but no one will dispute that bad publicity is something that politicians are always happy to grab on to and use to stir the political pot, seldom checking for accuracy. If keeping politicians properly informed was the only thing that public relations had done for the Air Force it would have been worth the effort.

The Air Force Systems Program Office had an office of information built in, which was run by Major Gerald Broening. By leaning on his right elbow, Major Broening could look into General Bellis' office. Nothing of any significance went on at the top of the program without Major Broening's knowing it. In fact, that was the purpose of the Information Office. Anything and everything was funneled into the SPO at Wright-Patterson Air Force Base, In Dayton, Ohio. If the press wanted information out at Edwards AFB, or wanted to talk to one of the subcontractors in the opposite corner of the United States, they would get the same answer: Clear it with the SPO Information Officer.

Major Broening's office in Dayton had a bank of telephones with which he could communicate to the Air Force world-wide. Down the hall was a room filled with communication equipment, some of which was secured for classified material. There was even a secured copier which could transmit classified copies of plans and data.

Since the elimination of the Total Package Procurement policy, Deputy Secretary of Defense Packard, under then Secretary of Defense Laird, advanced a prototype concept rather than a paper airplane study, and tied this prototype concept to the milestone concept. When the F-15 contract was signed on December 31, 1969, the terms, convenant, conditions and restrictions were spelled out in 146 pages which did not rely on the leap of faith letter of agreement that the Air Force had on the F-111 program.

The F-15 was the first airplane built after the institution of the "fly-before-buy" milestone approach to aircraft procurement. The F-15 program had 24 milestones, each of which had to be met before proceeding to the next one. There were financial incentives and penalties attached. The milestones involved, among others, the approval of the preliminary design review, the radar contractor selection, first flight, certain performance criteria, completion by the Air Force of its Category II aircraft test program, and ultimately the delivery of the first F-15 to the Tactical Air Command.

The contract called for certain incentives for meeting various milestones and deadlines on time and on or under budget. The management decision also called for using known technology whenever possible, or at the most a refinement of those known techniques. As a result, for example, by not requiring the inertial navigation to have drift error of one mile per hour, which would have cost much more money, but instead a three-mile drift error, the manufacturer used known state of the art and produced an inertial navigation computer that produced the one mile per hour drift anyway.

The Systems Program Office had within it smaller groups headed by program directorates. Airframe, avionics, tactical electronic warfare system (TEWS), and armament (while the Philco-Ford GAU-7 25mm gun was viable) reported directly to the System Program Director, General Bellis. The fifth program, the F100/F401 Joint Engine Project Office (JEPO) was a separate program, costing a third of the

The same computer that stores the design of the F-15 is used to cut these titanium bulkheads. The machine can mill four bulkheads at a time. *(McDonnell Douglas)*

Regardless of the sophistication, it still takes many man hours to put together the F-15. Notice in this picture the opening for the M-61 gun in the upper lefthand portion of the photo.

(McDonnell Douglas)

The fuselage appears as a rectangular housing for the two F-100 engines. The next step is for the wings to be joined. *(Flight International)*

MANUFACTURING BREAKDOWN
F-15 AIRCRAFT

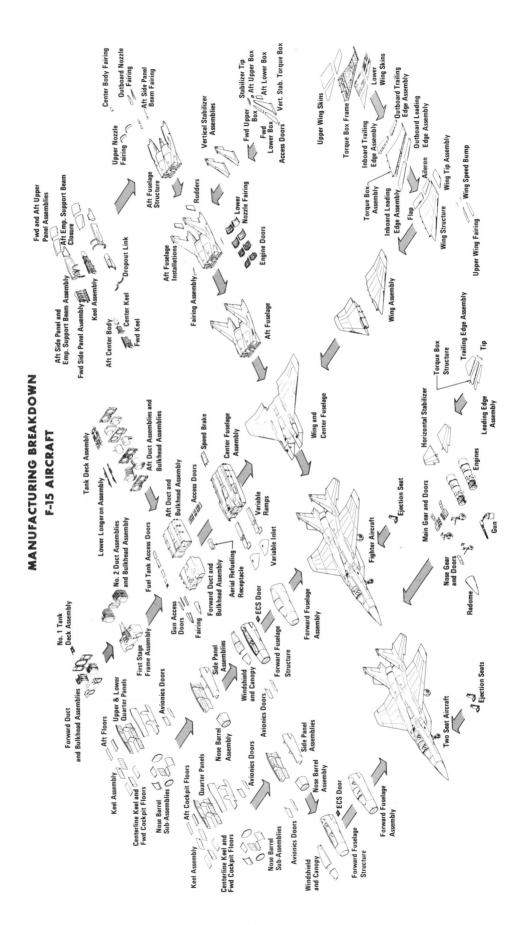

F-15 EAGLE MANUFACTURING BREAKDOWN

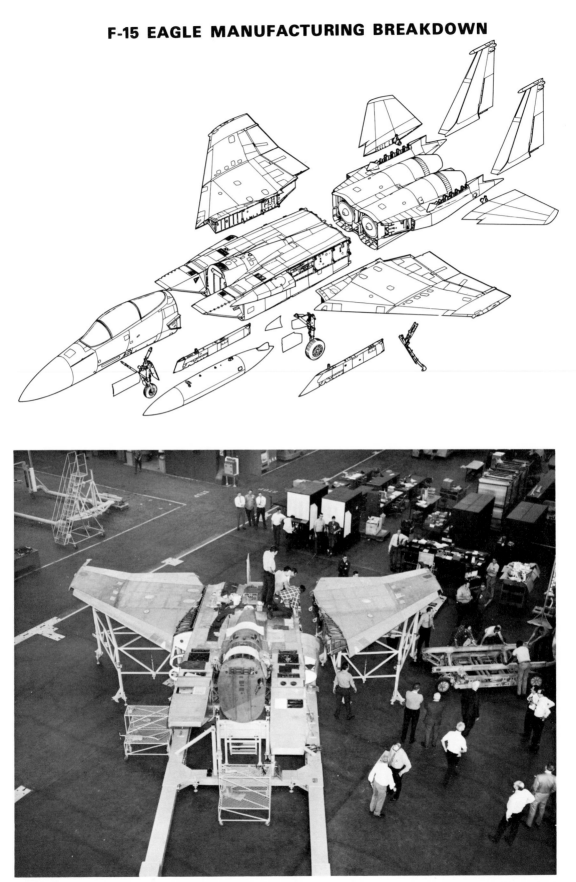

The wings are joined to the fuselage of the first F-15A.

(McDonnell Douglas)

This engineer is using Computer Aided Design (CAD). By touching two points in a computer-stored drawing, the engineer can command various shapes—lines, semi-circles, etc.—between those two points. Once the drawings are done, the same computer program can cut the metal for the aircraft without going through the process of drawing.   (McDonnell Douglas)

fabrication machinery. While the F-4 was 65 percent assembly and 35 percent fabrication, the F-15 has almost reversed those figures so that their fabrication takes 60 percent of the man hours and the assembly takes 40 percent. All of this resulted in the first production F-15, the 21st aircraft, taking 11,000 man hours in final assembly,while the first production F-4, the 48th aircraft, took a total of 35,000 man hours.

The use of the computer is another reason why the number of Engineering Change Proposals (ECP) were kept to a minimum. The F-4 had 135 ECPs before the first production aircraft flew while the F-15 had only 38. The gross weight often increases with these ECPs, and an increase in gross weight detracts from the performance of the aircraft, something no fighter pilot wants. Because the ECPs were kept to a minimum in the F-15, the weight increase from the first pre-production aircraft to the first production F-15—the 21st—was only 188 pounds, while the F-4 increased 3,050 pounds. For engines that together produced around 35,000 pounds of thrust, an increase of 3,050 pounds of weight would require a thrust increase of 10 percent alone to keep the thrust to weight what it was when the F-4 was first designed. Actually, the F-15 has lost weight since the program began. The first production single seat F-15A, serial number 73-085 (F-23) weighed 41,295 pounds. The 87th F-15 weighed 41,012 pounds, a reduction of 283 pounds.

McDonnell Douglas received a contract in May 1971 to develop a composite wing made of boron and other advanced aerospace techniques. By using those new techniques, the wing should be stronger, or at least as strong, with a reduction of 400 pounds per wing. The Air Force cancelled the project in February 1975, but the technology will be used in the AV-8B, and the F-18.

total development, but it still reported to General Bellis. These directorates also reported to General Bellis' counterpart at McDonnell Aircraft, Don Malvern, then vice president and general manager of the F-15 program.

The manufacturing of the F-15 is no small achievement. The F-15's production and design is aided by the computer. In fact, the

The test program is designed to make liars or saints out of the engineers. The test pilots on the F-15 flight test program worked in the company developed air combat simulator for months flying an "airplane" that the engineers claimed would fly like the real thing. After the first flight of the first F-15 on July 27, 1972, McDonnell Douglas Chief Test Pilot Irv Burrows said, "It was just like the simulator!"

Twenty pre-production F-15s were designated for the test program: 12 for contractor development and 8 for Air Force evaluation.

EFFECTIVE PRODUCTION WEIGHT CONTROL DEMONSTRATED

216 LB REDUCTION DURING 1975/1976

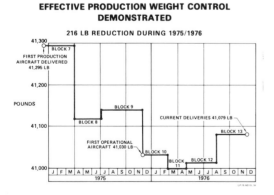

program is called Computer Aided Design (CAD) and Computer Aided Manufacturing (CAM). McDonnell Douglas software programs store programs with millions of bytes of data ready for recall for both the engineer and the

The first F-15, McAir F-1, stands at attention at the McDonnell Douglas test facility at Edwards AFB, California in July 1973. Unique to this photo is the collection of pre-production Category I F-15s. Notice the folded wings on USAF F-4 Phantoms. *(McDonnell Douglas)*

The Air Force had a Joint Test Force (JTF) made up of Tactical Air Command and Air Force Systems Command pilots. (Today JTF would include the contractor.) The test program was divided into three categories: Category I, now called Contractor Development, Test & Evaluation (CDT&E), was the responsibility of McDonnell Aircraft; Category II, now called Air Force Development, Test, & Evaluation (AFDT&E), belonged to the Air Force; and Category III, now called Follow on Operational Test & Evaluation (FOT&E), was the responsibility of the Air Force—initially with the Air Force Test and Evaluation Center (AFTEC) but ultimately with the 422nd Fighter Weapons

Squadron at Nellis AFB, Nevada.

McAir identifies all of their F-15s by number, so that the first F-15 is "F-1," the second "F-2," and the first TF-15 a two seat trainer version fully combat capable is "TF-1." The Category I test aircraft include F-1 through F-10 and the first two TFs. The Air Force Category II airplanes included the last 8 single seat F-15, but some of the Category I aircraft were transferred over to the Air Force when McAir was through with their programs. Even before the Air Force formally started its Category II program on March 14, 1974, it had been flying approximately 15 percent of the flights using McDonnell Douglas as a pre-arranged participation in the Category testing.

It is during the test flight program that suggestions are made to the engineers for improvement in the aircraft. The Engineering Change Proposals result from pilot investigation during the test programs. Only thirty-six ECPs had been recommended by the fall of 1974 and

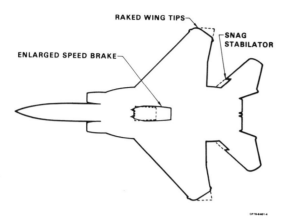

of these only 23 involved the aircraft. Twenty-one of these were incorporated in the first and second production aircraft, and the other two were incorporated into production aircraft number three. The ECPs that missed the first two production aircraft were minor in nature, involving only a bolt linkage and the re-routing of a wire bundle.

The most obvious changes are those made to the physical appearance of the F-15. The three observable changes are the enlarged speed brake, the raked wing tips, and the snagged stabilator. The original speedbrake caused a buffet at the desired drag configurations, so the newer brake, enlarged from 20 to 31.5 square feet was put in its place to create the needed drag at lower extension angles. The snagged stabilator was the solution to a flutter problem which was revealed in wind tunnel testing. By cutting the snag in the stabilator, a minor shift in the coefficient of pressure and a change in moment of inertia was satisfied. The snag was a production feature of the fourth F-15 (F-4) and was retrofitted to the first three pre-production aircraft (F-1, F-2, and F-3). The first F-15, F-1, was instrumented to test flying qualities and flutter. Early in the test program McAir discovered that there was an airloads problem and buffet problem on the wing at certain altitudes. In March, 1974, the McDonnell Douglas engineers at Edwards Air Force Base removed 4 square feet diagonally off the tip of F-4's wing to create the present raked appearance. A close examination of the wing tip shows the wood filler that McDonnell engineers used to test the new wing tip, which shows that there is a little of the wood and string left in modern aerodynamics.

There was another modification that was made early in the program, which did not involve a physical change in appearance. The landing gear, which is narrow by design, was not tolerant of cross winds with the control system and strut chamber design then in use. Modification to the strut (not visible) and several changes to the flight control system cleared the F-15 to 30 knots of crosswind.

The test program is responsible for keeping track of the amount of maintenance required on the F-15. One of the established design concepts that was issued in the original Request for Proposal (RFP) established that the Air Force wanted the F-15 to require the small amount of maintenance that the Army Air Corps experienced with the P-51 *Mustang*. The P-51 required approximately 15 maintenance man hours per flight hour (MMH/FH). The F-15 contract and RFP called for 11.3 MMH/FH at maturity for the F-15. To examine this—and other aspects of the program—a TF-15 (TF-2) flew to the Farnborough Air Show on August 26, 1974. The aircraft flew from Loring AFB, Maine, unrefueled to Bentwaters, England in 5.3 hours. In addition to visiting the Air Show, Col. Wendell Shawler, then the Air Force's F-15 JTF Director and first Air Force pilot to fly the F-15, and Irv Burrows, first to fly the F-15, visited some other

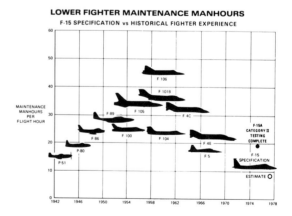

The history of maintenance man hours per flight hour is illustrated here to show where the F-15 falls historically. The MMH/FH is so good, that one Air Force general made an Air Force information officer omit the exact hours because the number was so low, that he felt it would be unbelievable.

(McDonnell Douglas)

Rollout ceremonies in May, 1972, show the first F-15A AFSN 71-280, McAir F-1. Notice the un-notched horizontal stabilator and the un-raked wing tips. The F-15 rollout was fourteen years after the first flight of the F-4 Phantom II, *on May 27, 1958. Only three visual changes were made to the appearance of this design: notched tail, clipped wing tips, and enlarged speedbrake.* (Flight International)

bases. They flew 92 demonstration hops in 43 days and had an impressive 4.25 MMH/FH, which would make any P-51 mechanic envious. Along with this maintainability and low MMH/FH that was made a contractual obligation, the Air Force called for a 30-minute requirement to change an engine. A McDonnell Douglas test team proved that the F-15 could meet this requirement by changing an engine in 18 minutes and 55 seconds. In doing this the company readily admitted that this quick time would not be what the average maintenance crew in the field would do, but it did demonstrate the maintainability principle that was designed into the F-15. Another requirement was a 12-minute combat turnaround time. The requirement called for 12 minutes to load the missiles, gun ammunition, liquid oxygen (LOX), fuel, oil service and make a quick in-

spection. McDonnell Douglas demonstrated the 12-minute requirement in 5 minutes and 50 seconds.

The F-15 was the first (and to date perhaps the only) aircraft accepting safety requirements in its contracts. It is probably no coincidence, then, that the F-15 is the only fighter to achieve its first 5,000 hours accident free. The first F-15 loss (serial No. 73-088) happened on October 15, 1975 by an Air Force pilot out of Luke Air Force Base. This first loss occurred after 7300 hours total flying time on 47 F-15s. By the end of 1976, F-15s had accumulated nearly 30,000 hours total flying time. A second F-15, Serial No. 74-129, was lost in early 1977 at ACEVAL/AIMVAL testing at Nellis AFB, Nevada when it collided with a Red Force F-5E.

The first accident resulted from the pilot turn-

Irv Burrows flies the first F-15 on its first flight, July 27, 1972, over Edwards AFB, California. Notice the squared off wing tips and the lack of a snag in the horizontal stabilator. The white blade antenna forward toward the aft end of the canopy is a secondary VHF back-up antenna for test communications.

(McDonnell Douglas)

ing off the generator switches because he had smoke in the cockpit. The boost pump in the main fuel tank went out as a result of these two generator switches being turned off, and the guesstimate was that the emergency generator, which runs an emergency boost pump to provide fuel to the engines, did not come on the line in time. At altitude this would have been no problem because F-100 engines have been air started before. However, this incident happened at low altitude, and since fan engines by nature are slow to start, the pilot had to eject.

The F-15 first flew on July 27, 1972. Since that time the F-15 has met all of its milestones on time with the exception of the F-100 engine which was several months late because of technical problems completing the durability tests. The Category I and II flight test program was completed with the delivery of the first production F-15 (TF-3) a TF-15A to Tactical Air Command at Luke Air Force Base on November 14, 1974. The following January the 19th pre-production aircraft (F-17) set eight climb-to-altitude records at Grand Forks Air Force Base. Six months later on 1 July 1975, the first Operational Tactical Air Command squadron—the 1st Tactical Fighter Wing (TFW)—was formed at Langley AFB, Virginia; and six months after the formation of the 1st TFW they received their first aircraft on 9 January 1976.

The first foreign country to take an interest in the F-15 was Iran which back in July 1973 examined the F-15 and the Grumman F-14 *Tomcat,* at Andrews Air Force Base. The Shah of Iran wanted to counter the MiG-25 *Foxbat* and at the time of his evaluation the F-14 and its *Phoenix* weapons system had demonstrated the capability to down the high flying *Foxbats.* The F-15s were in an earlier state of development and whether or not the AIM-7F had been demonstrated to the Shah is not known. Since that time the F-15 has publicly demonstrated capability to down a *Foxbat*-like target with its AIM-7Fs.

The Israelis came to Edwards Air Force Base in September 1974 to evaluate the F-15. Almost immediately they pushed the aircraft out

Chief Test Pilot Irv Burrows shows the Shah of Iran the F-15 at Andrews AFB, Maryland, during July 1973, approximately one year after the first flight. The politics that surrounded the selection of the F-14 Tomcat over the F-15 Eagle by the Shah is too complex and unsuitable for a book this short. Irv Burrows is to the left of the Shah, Major General Bellis, F-15 SPO Director, is to the right.

(McDonnell Douglas)

to the four corners of the flight envelope. One of the maneuvers that they used to test the response of the F-15 was to take off and make a climbing Immelman to 30,000 feet and dash out to 0.9 Mach in a minute and 40 seconds. It was also the Israelis who determined that the F-15 could fly a loop as slow as 150 knots.

The German Air Force made an evaluation in March 1975 and the Japanese Self Defense Force made two evaluations, one in June and July, 1975 and the second in May and June, 1976. TF-2 went to Canada and made two tours—one in June and the second in September 1975— to demonstrate the F-15's air superiority against Canadian CF-101s, CF-5s, and ECM equipped CF-100A and C's. The following month the United Kingdom evaluated the F-15 followed by a French evaluation the following April, 1976.

TF-2 made a trans-Pacific tour between October 6 and November 14, 1976. This 40 day trip logged 50 flights for a total flying time of 87.1 flight hours which was equivalent to flying 1.22 times around the world (26,378 nm-48,579 km). No flights were cancelled, and only one flight was delayed for about an hour. The TF-15 required an impressive 1.23 Maintenance Man Hours per Flight Hour. The *Eagle* had the distinction on this tour of being the first flight to fly nonstop and unrefueled across Australia.

Israel is the first country to transform its evaluation into acceptance of the F-15. Israel accepted the first four of 25 F-15s on December 11, 1976. The first four F-15s were pre-production aircraft, and were, ironically, F-14, F-15, F-16, and F-18.

What started out as a few concept formulation studies on the FX ended up as a 2.5 million manhour effort on a 37,500 page proposal which netted McDonnell Aircraft Company the F-15 contract number F33657-70-0300.

The F-15 flies with two CF-101B's during a visit to Canada. The CF-101B's were also designed and manufactured by McDonnell but represent 15-20 year older technology. (McDonnell Douglas)

The first production F-15 delivered to the Tactical Air Command at Luke AFB, Arizona, in November 1974. (McDonnell Douglas)

Lt. Col. Eitan Ben Eliyahu, Commanding Officer of the 133rd IAF Fighter Squadron, flies wing on the first two-seat F-15B Eagle delivered to Israel in December 1977. The Israelis bought the first four F-15s out of the pre-production Category II test aircraft. Within the first couple of months the Squadron was getting four flights per aircraft per day. With only four F-15s, within the first year the pilot with the lowest time in the F-15 had logged over 350 hours. The McAir cumulative number for the four F-15s sent to Israel were, ironically, F-14, F-15, F-16, and F-18. (McDonnell Douglas)

Shark-mouthed F-15A 71-0282 in Air Force Flight Dynamics Laboratory/Advanced Environmental Control System paint scheme at Edwards AFB, 11-20-77. *(Dennis Jenkins)*

An Air Force Test and Evaluation Center (AFTEC) F-15A flies with an ADCOM F-106 during Category III (FOT&E) evaluation. *(Spence Wilkinson)*

Two-place TF-15A (F-15B 71-0291) in French Air Force markings *before* demonstration flight at Edwards AFB, 4-27-76. *(Dennis Jenkins)*

Pre-production F-15, McAir Cume No. 4, AF Serial No. 71-0283 sits at Edwards AFB with typical pre-production paint, 5-20-73. The Air Superiority blue paint was flat (FS35450)on top and glossy (FS15450) on the bottom.*(Dennis Jenkins)*

An AFTEC F-15A (AFSN 73-107) with 57th FWW insignia on nacelle, Nellis AFB fin flash, and Luke AFB "LA" tail code, during Category III test and evaluation.
(Jim Rotramel)

A TF-15A (now F-15B) AFSN 73-112 of the 555 TFTS, 58 TFTW (58 TTW) sports black and white training stripes and the 12th Air Force Commander's number.
(Jim Rotramel)

An F-15A from the 461st TFTS at Luke AFB with red and white training stripes.
(Jim Rotramel)

The third in the series of colorful F-15s with paint scheme devised by Wing Commander Brig. Gen. Haeffner. AFSN 73-100 belongs to the 555 TFTS. This is the first grey airplane. The Federal Standard Numbers for the colors are: dark grey 36320, light grey 36375, with a 31.5% and 38.5% (spectral) visual reflectance respectively; green fin flash 14062; yellow 13538.
(Jim Rotramel)

35

Typical and unique F-15 tail markings.

1. *Pre-production paint scheme of air-superiority blue and day-glow tail and wing markings. (Dennis Jenkins).* 2. *Horizontal fin flash belongs to the 57th FWW (now TTW) and the tail code to 58th TFTW (now TTW). This code/fin flash was unique to AFTEC. Category III (FOT&E) aircraft of 422 FWS now have "WA" tail code. (Don Logan)* 3. *Typical 555 TFTS tail. (Dennis Jenkins)* 4. *Tail of 461 TFTS. (Jim Rotramel)* 5. *Paint scheme of Brig. Gen. Haeffner, 58th TFTW Wing Commander. (Dennis Jenkins)* 6. *12th Air Force Com-*

mander's F-15. (Dennis Jenkins) 7. *Gen. Haeffner's F-15 in Ferris paint scheme. (Dennis Jenkins)* 8. *36th TFW tail with no fin flash. (M. France)* 9. *1st TFW tail of 71st TFS. 27th TFS has yellow, and 94th TFS has blue fin flash. (Ray Leader)* 10. *Tail of Advanced Environmental Control System F-15. Insignia is of Air Force Flight Dynamics Laboratory. Near vertical stripe is an experimental position for formation flight not on production aircraft. (Dennis Jenkins)*

36

F-15 vs F-4
SIZE COMPARISON

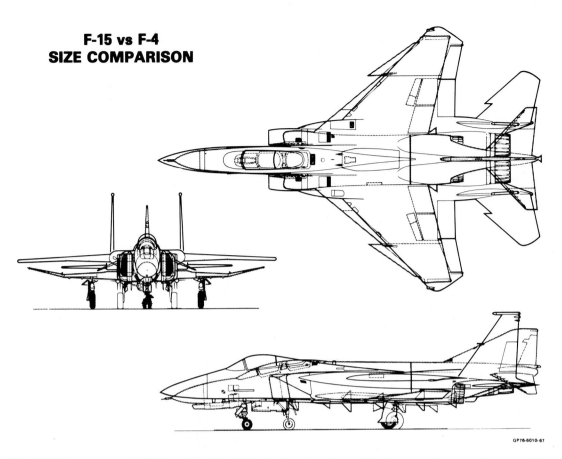

GP76-6010-67

The F-15 is compared with the size of the F-4. On the top view notice how much more wing area the F-15 has. Notice also the size of the tail surfaces necessary for maneuverability. The side view shows how the fuselage falls away from the rearward line-of-sight for better visibility. Notice, too, the difference in landing gear stance from both the side and front. (McDonnell Douglas)

External View

The twin vertical tail that became the mark of the MiG-25 *Foxbat* is becoming more common with today's air superiority fighters, and the F-15 *Eagle* is no exception. This twin vertical tail design has two major benefits: it provides yaw stability at high speeds and high angle of attack. The F-15 originally had a shorter vertical clearance, with the addition of a ventral fin, but this design was dropped because it caused cruise drag.

A common question asked is, why doesn't the F-15 have variable sweep? At first glance variable sweep seems to be a more modern state of the art, especially when comparing the Russian trend which has made their more recent fighters all with variable sweep wings. While it is true that variable geometry does solve many problems aerodynamically, it does create additional cost, weight, and maintenance problems. The main function of the variable sweep wing is to expand the aircraft envelope, and enlarge the point design area so that the aircraft is optimized for a larger area in

the flight envelope. However, there are other solutions as evidenced by the F-15.

The Air Force's evaluation of the dogfights in Southeast Asia led them to believe that most dogfights take place between .6 and 1.2 Mach, and below 30,000 feet. Accordingly, the F-15 was designed for that arena, disregarding the benefits of forward sweeping wings which would allow for a long loiter and endurance time. (Long loiter time was solved another way through the FAST Pack system mentioned below.)

The F-15 is about the same size as the F-4 *Phantom,* but weighs 6,000 pounds less than the F-4E at full combat gross takeoff weight. This is a function of the titanium and composite technology in the materials used to built the aircraft and attention to subsystem design. The amount of titanium and other composites is considered a conservative approach with its 26 percent titanium, when compared with over 90 percent titanium YF-12 and SR-71 technology of almost a decade earlier.

37

This chart shows the increased visibility from the F-15 cockpit compared to the F-4.

One of the greatest assets a fighter pilot can have is good visibility. The unobstructed forward visibility speaks for itself with McAir test pilot Bill Brinks at the controls. Air Force pilots were quick to notice the Naval Test Pilot School patch on the right shoulder. *(McDonnell Douglas)*

The F-15 is the first USAF fighter since the F-86 Sabre to have unobstructed rearward visibility.
(McDonnell Douglas)

The rectangular inlets which pivot at the base are the only variable geometry on the F-15, and are a first for a fighter aircraft. When the F-15 increases its angle of attack, the pivoting inlet permits the air to enter the engine at a less radical deflection angle. The intake also acts as a canard because of its area and position in front of the center of aerodynamic pressure. Subsonically, it contributes 10 percent and supersonically 30 percent effectiveness to the horizontal tails, which allowed for a reduction in size and a saving of about 180 pounds. All of this activity around the inlet is controlled by the air inlet control, part of the overall central computer.

Interceptor aircraft never required fishbowl canopies. As long as there was good forward visibility, the designers tried to keep the design of the aircraft as aerodynamically streamlined as possible.

The F-15's mission requires that the pilot have excellent visibility, and that is what he has. When the canopy closes for the first time on a pilot who is used to flying F-4 *Phantoms*, the

VARIABLE INLET
REDUCES REQUIRED BYPASS AREA

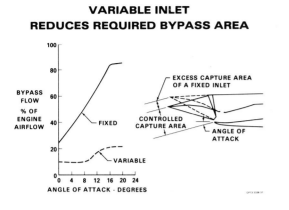

LATERAL CONTROL SYSTEM

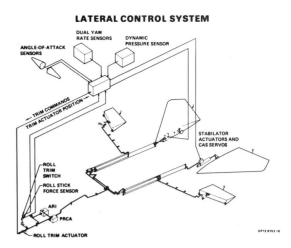

comments range from ecstatic to euphoric. Not only does the design of the canopy go back to the days of World War II and P-51 *Mustangs*, it adds a new dimension—downward. The canopy actually bulges out at the sides, and this combined with the low canopy rail creates the feeling of flying in the open. Adding to this feeling is the single piece windshield and almost single piece canopy. The material the canopy is made of does not come in sheets large enough for one continuous piece, so aft of the pilot the canopy is pieced together. The cockpit is raised structurally so that it is the highest point of the plane, disregarding the vertical stabilizers.

Flight Controls

The flight control system in the F-15 appears to be complicated but in reality is nothing more than two systems imposed upon each other. One is made up of a hydro-mechanical linkage and the other is a hydro-electrical linkage. Primary flight control is achieved with the hydro-electrical linkage since it provides the best possible handling qualities. If battle damage affects the mechanical linkage there is little effect to the flight controls.

The primary control surfaces in the F-15 include the outboard ailerons, which have a 20° movement up or down, horizontal stabilators which move symmetrically for pitch and differentially for additional roll control, and twin rudders on the vertical stabilators. The aircraft rolls with ailerons and differential stabilators with mechanical flight controls, but with stabilators only with electrical inputs.

The A-4 is probably the last of the high performance jet aircraft that still has direct cable linkage to the flight controls with no hydraulic or mechanical actuator. Direct linkage is common in slower performing aircraft, but at high

speeds, the amount of force needed to deflect the surfaces to make the desired changes in flight path cannot be accomplished with man power alone. Consequently, the F-15 like other high performance jet aircraft has hydraulic actuators that deflect the flight surfaces. What is unique about the system are the two different signals—mechanical or electrical—that tell these actuators what to do.

LONGITUDINAL CONTROL SYSTEM

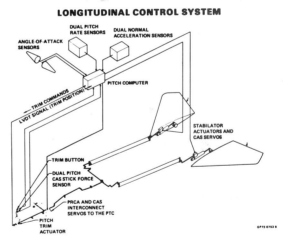

The Automatic Flight Control System (AFCS) has two major jobs within the flight control arena: provide the Control Augmentation System (CAS) and the functions normally associated with an autopilot. The CAS is the primary control system for the F-15 in that it is the CAS that provides the electric inputs to the control surfaces. The CAS senses the pitch, roll, and yaw rates; vertical and lateral acceleration; angle of attack, and provides the proper inputs for the particular speed and *g* forces. This function relieves the pilot of a fatigue problem which he might otherwise face by having to constantly compensate for increases and decreases in control surface

39

pressure.

The hydraulic system that runs the flight controls consists of three independent systems—two main systems and a backup. One system controls the right aileron, right rudder, and the left and right differential stabilators. The other main system controls the left aileron, left rudder, and the left and right differential stabilators. The backup system is the Utility Hydraulic System. It normally provides power for the landing gear, brakes, steering, variable inlet ramps, radar antenna, and other components. In the event of the loss of power from either of the two main independent systems, the Utility Hydraulic System will act as a backup for the ailerons, rudders and differential stabilators.

The original aircraft canopy had a one piece windshield made from polycarbonate (Lexan) which could tolerate 315° F. The current material is stretched acrylic which can tolerate bird strikes (4 pounds) up to 335 knots. It can withstand up to 60 knots relative wind in the open position on the ground.

The airframe is mainly conventional stringer, longeron, and frame bulkhead design. The major bulkheads are titanium, with both titanium and aluminum used for skins, stringers and frames. Some of the more exotic materials are in the vertical stabilizer and horizontal stabilators. The spars are titanium filled with honeycomb, but then covered with boron-epoxy skin, with the rudder being covered with graphite and epoxy, and speed brake covered with graphite.

Internal

In addition to the visibility, the F-15 pilot gets another surprise when he sits in the cockpit for the first time—environmental controls that rival any modern office building. Multimillion dollar jet aircraft consistently taxi with their canopies open. This is not true of the F-15. On a hot day at Luke Air Force Base when the temperature is over 100° the F-15 flight crews taxi with their canopies down to keep in the air-conditioning. The system is so effective that the temperature drops down from over 100° to 72° within a couple of minutes. The cabin pressurization schedule calls for a constant cabin altitude of 8,000 feet up to 23,100 feet. Above this altitude the regulator maintains a 5 PSI differential between cabin and outside pressure. At 40,000 feet the cockpit would be 15,500 and at 65,000 feet the cabin altitude would be around 24,000 feet.

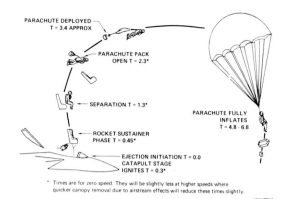

The ejection seat sequence times for the F-15 at zero airspeed. The time will be slightly less at higher speeds where quicker canopy removal due to airstream effects will reduce these times slightly. *(McDonnell Douglas)*

The ejection seat is a Douglas Aircraft Co. ESCAPC IC-7. The seat is effective from 0 to 600 knots equivalent airspeed (KEAS) at ground level. The seat has a Directional Automatic Realignment of Trajectory (DART) system that stabilizes the seat during rocket burn.

The F-15 carries 11,635 pounds of fuel internally but will carry 2,000 more internally in the near future. The fuel system is designed to work automatically. Internally the aircraft has 6 tanks: 4 fuselage and 2 wing tanks. The engine feed tanks all contain foam in varying amounts to minimize damage from projectiles up to 50 caliber. All of the tanks have reticulated foam which suppresses fire and explosion. The transfer from the three 600 gallon external tanks to the internal tanks is automatic and does not require pilot attention.

The cockpit is simpler than the F-4 with 30 percent fewer gauges and nothing that is needed in flight behind the pilot's elbows. Two noticeable features are the Head Up Display (HUD) and the communication radio and Identification Friend or Foe (IFF). The HUD is the primary flight instrument. The radio, which in the past has required pilots to look down on the side panel (often during critical workloads) to change frequency, is now just below the HUD. This new position requires only the slightest eye movement to change frequency channels.

The location of the various radios, armament panels, fuel gauges, etc., are self-explanatory when viewing the illustration of the cockpit on pages 50-51. The use and purpose of most of the avionics and weapons systems will be covered in the section on weapons and avionics.

F-15A
PRODUCTION EAGLE PACKAGE
(PEP-2000)

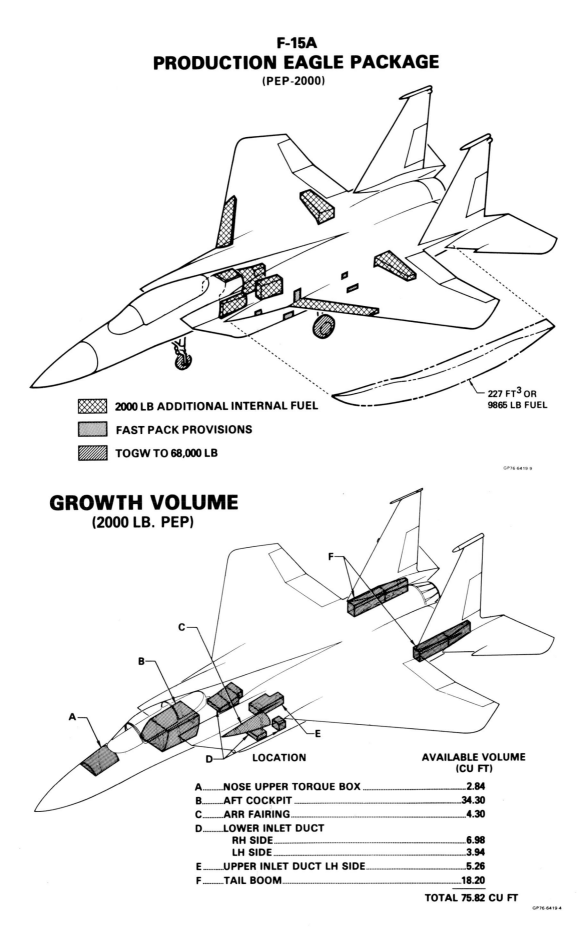

227 FT³ OR 9865 LB FUEL

⊠ **2000 LB ADDITIONAL INTERNAL FUEL**

▨ **FAST PACK PROVISIONS**

▨ **TOGW TO 68,000 LB**

GP76-6419-9

GROWTH VOLUME
(2000 LB. PEP)

LOCATION	AVAILABLE VOLUME (CU FT)
A......NOSE UPPER TORQUE BOX	2.84
B......AFT COCKPIT	34.30
C......ARR FAIRING	4.30
D......LOWER INLET DUCT	
RH SIDE	6.98
LH SIDE	3.94
E......UPPER INLET DUCT LH SIDE	5.26
F......TAIL BOOM	18.20

TOTAL 75.82 CU FT

GP76-6419-4

McDonnell Douglas F-15A Eagle

Notable features in this Eagle presentation by "Flight" artist Mike Badrocke are the mechanically simple near-delta wing; the "nodding" engine air-intakes; the very large speed brake (rapid deceleration in combat can be as essential as high power-to-weight); the 20mm cannon in the starboard wing-root balanced by the recessed flight-refuelling receptacle in the port wing; the AMAD (aircraft-mounted accessory drive) system for ancillaries such as hydraulic pumps and electrical generators; the twin-boom rear-fuselage configuration carrying the empennage; the empty compartment for the second crew member; the convergent/divergent engine nozzles to minimise base- and boat-tail drag; and the configuration of the new AIM-9L Sidewinder.

KEY

Structure and general
1 Glassfibre radome, hinged to starboard
2 Birdproof frameless windshield, diffusion-bonded acrylic material
3 Boarding ladder
4 Step/handhold
5 Canopy seal
6 Canopy counterbalance strut
7 Jettison strut
8 Emergency opening lever (external)
9 McDonnell Douglas Escapac IC-7 ejection seat
10 Seat arming lever
11 Space provision for second crew-member's seat (TF-15A)
12 Rear-view mirrors
13 Standby compass
14 Machined fuselage frames (aluminium)
15 Machined fuselage frames (titanium)
16 Titanium aft-fuselage structure
17 Fin/tailplane support boom
18 Titanium fin spars
19 Boron-composite skin on aluminium-honeycomb core
20 Aluminium skin on Nomex-honeycomb core
21 Steel leading-edge member
22 Tailplane mounting trunnion
23 Machined tailplane-spar attachment fitting
24 Machined titanium wing spars with fuel sealing injected through channels in spar-skin joint
25 Spar/fuselage upper and lower pin joints
26 Aluminium front spar
27 Light-alloy fixed-leading-edge structure
28 Trailing-edge support link
29 Titanium lower skin (inboard)
30 Aluminium lower skin (outboard)
31 Aluminium upper skins
32 Skin splice
33 Integrally machined L-section stringers
34 Machined ribs
35 Pylon support fittings
36 Honeycomb control surfaces
37 Control-surface piano hinges on lower skin
38 Pitot head
39 Angle-of-attack sensor
40 Total temperature probe

Air systems
A1 Bleed-air supply from engines
A2 Primary heat-exchangers (each side)
A3 Intake duct bleed-air plenum (primary cooling air)
A4 Primary heat-exchanger exhaust
A5 Bleed-air crossfeed duct
A6 Primary air supply to air cycle air conditioning subsystem (ACACS)
A7 ACACS compartment
A8 Boundary-layer cooling-air inlet
A9 Cabin heat-exchanger
A10 Cooling-air exhaust
A11 Cabin-conditioning air-supply duct
A12 Windscreen de-misting duct
A13 Equipment cooling-air supply
A14 Cabin pressure-relief and outflow valves

Controls
C1 Control column with stick-force transducers
C2 Aileron and elevator rod linkage
C3 Pitch/roll channel assembly (PRCA)
C4 Aileron/rudder interconnect unit (ARI)
C5 Cable drive to aileron and elevator quadrants
C6 Aileron actuator
C7 Tailplane actuator (pitch control, and roll control at high angles of attack)
C8 Hydraulic rotary actuator for rudder
C9 Bowden-type cable to rudder actuator
C10 Plain flaps
C11 Hydraulic flap actuator (to be replaced by electrical actuation from production aircraft No 42)
C12 Airbrake
C13 Airbrake actuator
C14 Locating spigot

Electrics and electronics
E1 40/50kVA generators (two)
E2 Emergency generator, hydraulically powered
E3 Landing/taxi lights
E4 Navigation lights
E5 Collision beacon
E6 Variable-intensity formation lights
E7 Radar scanner, Hughes APG-63 pulse-Doppler radar
E8 IFF array
E9 Flood horn radar aerial
E10 ILS glideslope aerial
E11 UHF, Tacan, ILS marker-beacon aerials beneath fuselage
E12 Upper UHF/IFF aerial
E13 Upper Tacan aerial
E14 Forward equipment bay, port, containing radar processor, radar power supply, radar data processor, radar transmitters and receivers, and RF oscillator
E15 Forward equipment bay, starboard, containing flight director, flight control computers, air-data computer, interrogator transceiver, target data processor, and Tacan, ADF, UHF and ILS
E16 Lower equipment bay, containing HUD and VSD signal-processors, digital computer, stores station controller, converter programmer and liquid-oxygen container and evaporator mounted in starboard bay
E17 Ground-test panel
E18 Tactical electronic warfare system (Tews) equipment
E19 Tews antennas (radar warning etc.)

Fuel
F1 Wing integral fuel tank
F2 Reticulated foam filling
F3 Fuel vent box
F4 Transfer pumps and lines
F5 Wing/fuselage tank transfer pipes
F6 Vent line
F7 Fuselage bag-type tanks
F8 Feed tank for starboard engine with boost pump
F9 Feed tank for port engine with boost pump
F10 Tank access panels
F11 Fuel delivery to engines
F12 Flying-boom-type in-flight refuelling adaptor
F13 Adaptor door opening and emergency opening actuators
F14 Fuel vent and dump line

Hydraulics
H1 Power control systems Nos 1 and 2 pumps, 3,000lb/sq in
H2 Utility pumps
H3 Emergency generator pump
H4 Jet-fuel main engine starter initiated by run-up accumulators
H5 Radar scanner actuating motors
H6 Gun drive unit

Air-intake system
I1 Variable-capture-area air intake
I2 Intake pivot
I3 Mechanically linked ramps
I4 Diffuser ramp
I5 Ramp actuators
I6 Bypass door
I7 Boundary-layer bleed-air holes on inner surfaces

Michael J. Badrocke ARAeS M.S.I.A.
St. Louis, 75

18 Bleed-air exit louvres
19 Intake pressure sensor
I10 Intake control computer
I11 Intake trunking

Powerplant
P1 Pratt & Whitney F100-PW-100 turbofan engines
P2 Engine-mounting trunnion each side
P3 Front support link
P4 Engine-mounting access door
P5 Borescope inspection door
P6 Augmenter duct
P7 Convergent/divergent nozzle

P8 "Fueldraulic" nozzle actuators (five per engine)
P9 Engine-bay firewalls
P10 Fire-suppression bottle
P11 Engine-bay venting air
P12 Power take-off shaft
P13 Airframe-mounted accessory drive (AMAD) linked gearboxes
P14 Jet-fuel main engine starter

Stores pylons and weapons
S1 Centre-fuselage stores pylon
S2 600 US gal fuel tank
S3 Inboard wing pylon
S4 AIM-9L Sidewinder air-to-air missile
S5 Triple ejector rack
S6 500lb general-purpose bombs
S7 Outboard pylon
S8 Westinghouse ECM pod, outboard pylon can also carry target-designator pod
S9 AIM-7F Sparrow III air-to-air missiles
S10 Recessed launch/adapter unit
S11 M61A-1 20mm six-barrel rotary cannon, boresighted to cross line of sight at 2,250ft
S12 Cannon mounting link
S13 Cannon driveshaft
S14 Ammunition-feed/link-return chutes
S15 Ammunition drum

Undercarriage
U1 Forward-retracting steerable nosewheel
U2 Forward-retracting mainwheel unit
U3 Multi-plate disc-brake and anti-skid unit
U4 Mainwheel retraction well beneath intake trunk
U5 Main-leg jacking point for individual wheel changing
U6 Airfield arrester-hook pivot mounting

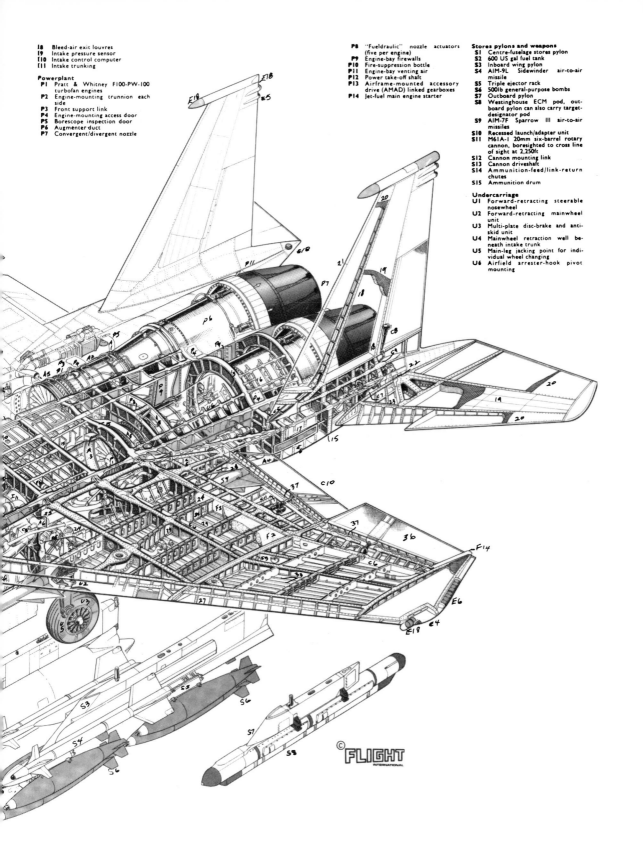

© FLIGHT INTERNATIONAL

F-15 Paint Schemes

Compass Ghost Grey

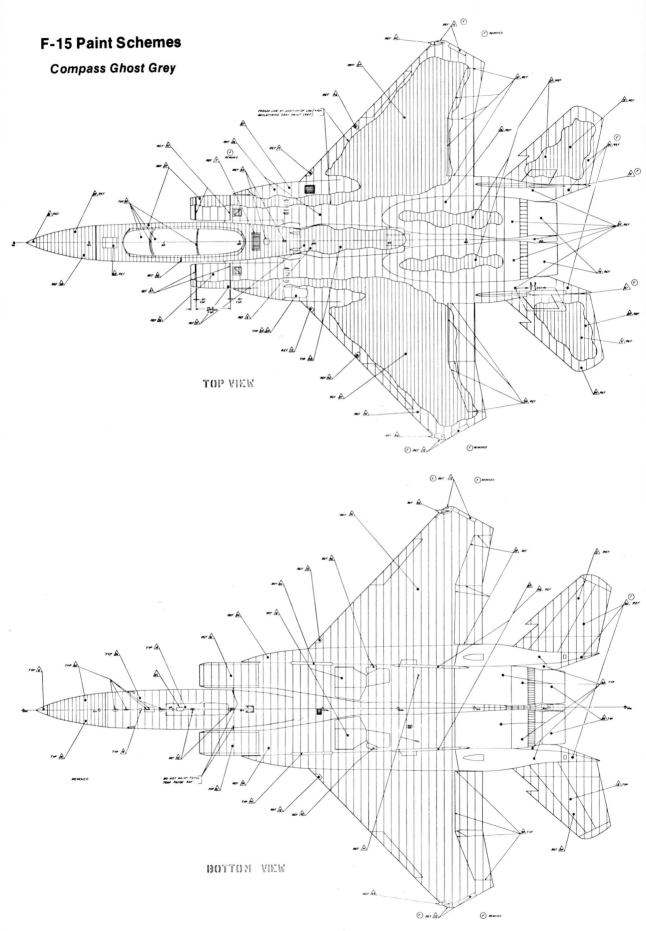

TOP VIEW

BOTTOM VIEW

44

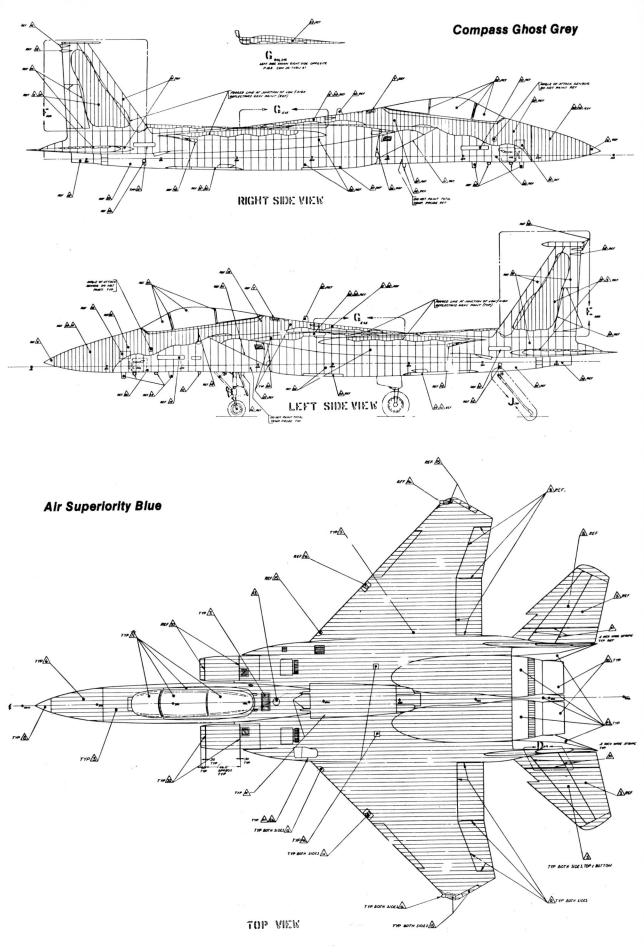

Compass Ghost Grey

RIGHT SIDE VIEW

LEFT SIDE VIEW

Air Superiority Blue

TOP VIEW

45

Air Superiority Blue

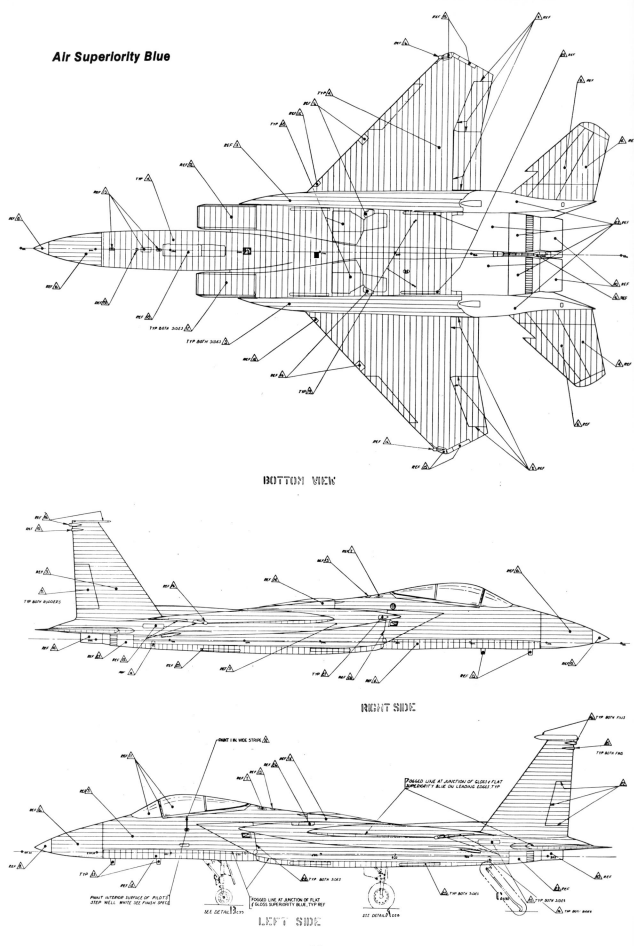

BOTTOM VIEW

RIGHT SIDE

LEFT SIDE

Paint Scheme Legend

* ASTERISK INDICATES FLAG NOTE ....

1 GENERAL FINISH IN ACCORDANCE WITH 68A900000

2 EXTERNAL FINISH APPLIED IN ACCORDANCE WITH PS13646. ALL EXTERNAL PAINT SHALL BE MMS-420 ALIPHATIC POLYURETHANE SYSTEM

* 3 UPPER SURFACE OF AIRCRAFT EXCEPT AS NOTED- APPLY MMS-420 ALIPHATIC POLYURETHANE FINISH SYSTEM COLOR FLAT SUPERIORITY BLUE PER PS13646

* 4 LOWER SURFACE OF AIRCRAFT EXCEPT AS NOTED- APPLY MMS-420 ALIPHATIC POLYURETHANE FINISH SYSTEM COLOR GLOSS SUPERIORITY BLUE PER PS13646

* 5 PAINT COMPOSITE SKINS PER PS13646

* 6 DO NOT PAINT NOSE RADOME. THIS ITEM FINISHED AT VENDOR. TOUCH UP NOSE RADOME SAME COLOR AS AIRCRAFT PER PS13646. PAINT SHEET METAL NOSE RADOMES WITH MMS-420 ALIPHATIC POLYURETHANE FINISH SYSTEM COLOR FLAT SUPERIORITY BLUE PER PS13646

* 7 DO NOT PAINT SECONDARY HEAT EXCHANGER LOUVRE

* 8 DO NOT PAINT RADOME BOOT

* 9 PAINT CUTOUT AREAS IN WING AND MATING ENCLOSURE AREAS OF FLAPS AND AILERONS FLAT SUPERIORITY BLUE PER PS13646

* 10 ENGINE EXHAUST NOZZLES, DO NOT PAINT

* 11 DO NOT PAINT CANOPY OR WINDSHIELD FIBERGLASS EDGING STRIPS. PAINT EXTERIOR SURFACE OF METAL FRAME FLAT SUPERIORITY BLUE PER PS13646

* 12 PAINT INTERIOR MOLDLINE SURFACE OF ENGINE AIR INTAKE DUCT FROM LEADING EDGE OF DUCT TO AFT END OF THIRD RAMP GLOSS SUPERIORITY BLUE PER PS13646. PAINT INTERIOR MOLDLINE DUCT SURFACE FROM AFT END OF THIRD RAMP TO F.S. 626 COLOR NO 17875 INSIGNIA WHITE PER PS13646

* 13 ANTENNAS PAINTED AT VENDOR. APPLY MMS-420 ALIPHATIC POLYURETHANE ENAMEL. COLOR FLAT OR GLOSS SUPERIORITY BLUE AS APPLICABLE PER PS13646 TO MATCH SURROUNDING AREA. DO NOT PAINT OVER ANTENNAS WHICH ALREADY MATCH SURROUNDING AREA COLOR AND GLOSS

* 14 PAINT SPEED BRAKE WELL AND INNER SURFACE OF SPEED BRAKE FLAT SUPERIORITY BLUE PER PS13646

15 DO NOT PAINT LENS PORTION OF LIGHTS

16 RADOMES PAINTED AT VENDOR. DO NOT PAINT

17 REMOVED

* 18 PAINT INTERIOR SURFACE OF WELLS AND DOORS INSIGNIA WHITE

* 19 KEEP JACK PAD HOLES FREE OF PAINT. COAT WITH MIL-G-81322 GREASE

* 20 MAIN AND NOSE LANDING GEAR WHEELS PAINTED BY VENDOR. TOUCH UP AS REQUIRED WITH MIL-L-19537 ACRYLIC LACQUER, COLOR NO 17038 GLOSS BLACK

* 21 MAIN AND NOSE LANDING GEAR PAINTED BY VENDOR. TOUCH UP AS REQUIRED WITH MMS-420 ALIPHATIC POLYURETHANE ENAMEL, COLOR NO 17875 INSIGNIA WHITE PER PS13646

* 22 PAINT CUTOUT AREAS OF VERTICAL FIN AND MATING RUDDER ENCLOSURE AREA FLAT SUPERIORITY BLUE PER PS13646

* 23 DO NOT PAINT UPPER AND LOWER NOZZLE FAIRING DOORS, SIDEWALL FAIRING, AFT SIDEWALL FAIRING /BLK 1 THRU BLK 11/, CENTERBODY FAIRING ASSEMBLY, AND AREAS AS SHOWN

24 TOUCH UP PAINT IN COCKPIT AS REQUIRED WITH MMS-420 ALIPHATIC POLYURETHANE ENAMEL PER PS13646

* 25 DO NOT PAINT AFT MISSILE WELLS

* 26 DO NOT PAINT AERIAL REFUELING RECEPTACLE WELL, THIS WILL RECEIVE THE MMS-425 PRIMER ONLY

* 27 PAINT INTERIOR OF GUN COMPARTMENT INSIGNIA WHITE COLOR NO 17875 PER PS13646

* 28 DO NOT OVERCOAT TEFLON FILLED ANTI-CHAFE COATING ON ENGINE AIR INTAKE DUCT AND SCOOP SKINS

* 29 PAINT ARRESTING HOOK WITH ALTERNATING 4 INCH BANDS OF COLOR NO 17875 INSIGNIA WHITE AND NO 37038 BLACK MMS-420 ALIPHATIC POLYURETHANE ENAMEL PER PS13646. DO NOT PAINT HOOK POINT

30 APPLY .50 WIDE BORDER WITH GRAY COLOR NO. 16307 PER PS13646

31 REMOVED

* 32 PAINT ONE /1/ INCH WIDE STRIPE FROM CENTERLINE OF STEP UP TO THE CANOPY SILL, COLOR NO. 16307 /GRAY/ PER FED. STANDARD 595. APPLY PER PS13646

33 LAST VIEW LETTER USED IS K

* 34 DO NOT PAINT THE MOLD LINE SURFACE OF THE INFLIGHT REFUELING SLIPWAY DOORS. THESE DOORS WILL CONTINUE TO RECEIVE THE MMS420 FINISH SYSTEM. EFF. F-15A CUM 14&UP, TF-15A CUM 3&UP

35 FOR ALL ARMAMENT AND EXTERNAL FUEL TANKS PAINT MATERIAL AND COLOR SEE THE FOLLOWING DRAWINGS. 68A000016 /EXTERNAL FUEL TANKS/, 68A000018 /CENTERLINE PYLON/, 68A000019 /INBOARD PYLON/, 68A000020 /OUTBOARD PYLON/, 68A000023 /AIM-9 ADAPTER/ 68A000024 /AIM-7F LAUNCHER/, 68A730081 /MER200 DESIGN SPEC./

* 36 PAINT WITH MMS-420 ALIPHATIC POLYURETHANE FINISH SYSTEM, FED-STD 595 COLOR NO. 36375 COMPASS GHOST GRAY /LIGHT GRAY/ PER PS13646

* 37 PAINT WITH MMS-420 ALIPHATIC POLYURETHANE FINISH SYSTEM, FED-STD 595 COLOR NO. 36320 COMPASS GHOST GRAY /DARK GRAY/ PER PS13646

* 38 DO NOT PAINT NOSE RADOME. THIS ITEM FINISHED AT VENDOR. TOUCH UP AS REQUIRED PER PS13646. PAINT RADOME WITH MMS-420 ALIPHATIC POLYURETHANE FINISH SYSTEM. COLOR- LOW REFLECTANCE GRAY /DARK GRAY/, REFINISH BLUE RADOMES PER PS13646

* 39 PAINT CUTOUT AREAS IN WING AND MATING ENCLOSURE AREAS OF FLAPS AND AILERONS LOW REFLECTANCE GRAY /DARK GRAY/

* 40 DO NOT PAINT CANOPY OR WINDSHIELD TRANSPARENCIES OR FIBERGLASS EDGING STRIPS. PAINT EXTERIOR SURFACE OF METAL FRAME LOW REFLECTANCE GRAY /DARK GRAY/ PER PS13646

* 41 PAINT INTERIOR MOLDLINE SURFACE OF ENGINE AIR INTAKE DUCT FROM LEADING EDGE OF DUCT TO AFT END OF DIFFUSER RAMP HIGH REFLECTANCE GRAY /LIGHT GRAY/ PER PS13646. PAINT INTERIOR MOLDLINE DUCT SURFACE FROM AFT END OF DIFFUSER RAMP TO FS626.00 INSIGNIA WHITE COLOR NO. 17875 PER PS13646

* 42 ANTENNAS AND RADOMES PAINTED AT VENDOR, DO NOT OVERCOAT. REFINISH BLUE ANTENNAS AND RADOMES TO MATCH GRAY SURROUNDING AREAS PER PS13646

* 43 PAINT SPEEDBRAKE WELL AND UNDERSIDE OF SPEEDBRAKE HIGH REFLECTANCE GRAY /LIGHT GRAY/ PER PS13646

44 REMOVED

* 45 PAINT CUTOUT AREAS OF VERTICAL FIN AND MATING RUDDER ENCLOSURE AREA HIGH REFLECTANCE GRAY /LIGHT GRAY/ PER PS13646

* 46 MISSILE WELLS SHOWN WITH LAUNCHERS REMOVED

* 47 APPLY .50 WIDE FLAT BLACK STRIPE, COLOR NO. 37038 PER PS13646

* 48 PAINT ONE /1/ INCH WIDE STRIPE FROM CENTERLINE OF STEP UP TO THE CANOPY SILL, FLAT BLACK COLOR NO. 37038 PER FED. STD. 595 APPLY PER PS13646

* 49 DO NOT PAINT

50 PRIME ALL TITANIUM AND CORROSION RESISTANT /ML/ SURFACES WITH MMS405 EPOXY PRIMER PER PS13646, F-15A CUM 44&UP, TF-15A CUM 11&UP, EXCEPT THOSE AREAS DESIGNATED TO BE UNPAINTED

* 51 PAINT L & R HORIZONTAL STABILATOR CLOSURE RIBS & MATING AREAS ON AFT FUSELAGE HIGH REFLECTANCE GRAY, /LIGHT GRAY/, TO MATCH SURROUNDING AREA

FUSELAGE SECTIONS

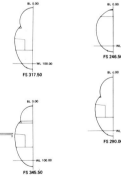

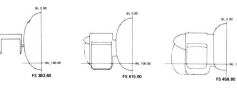
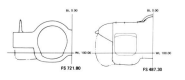
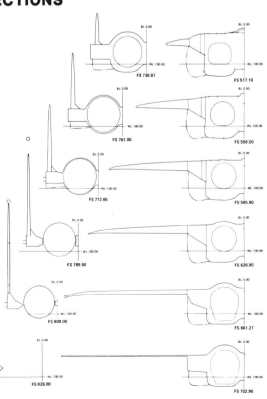

FS 317.50
FS 246.50
BL 0.00 WL 100.00
FS 130.50
FS 174.00
FS 207.65
FS 345.50
FS 290.00
FS 383.60
FS 415.00
FS 458.80
FS 721.80
FS 487.30
FS 738.87
FS 517.10
FS 761.00
FS 558.50
FS 772.65
FS 595.90
FS 789.50
FS 626.90
FS 809.00
FS 661.27
FS 826.00
FS 702.90

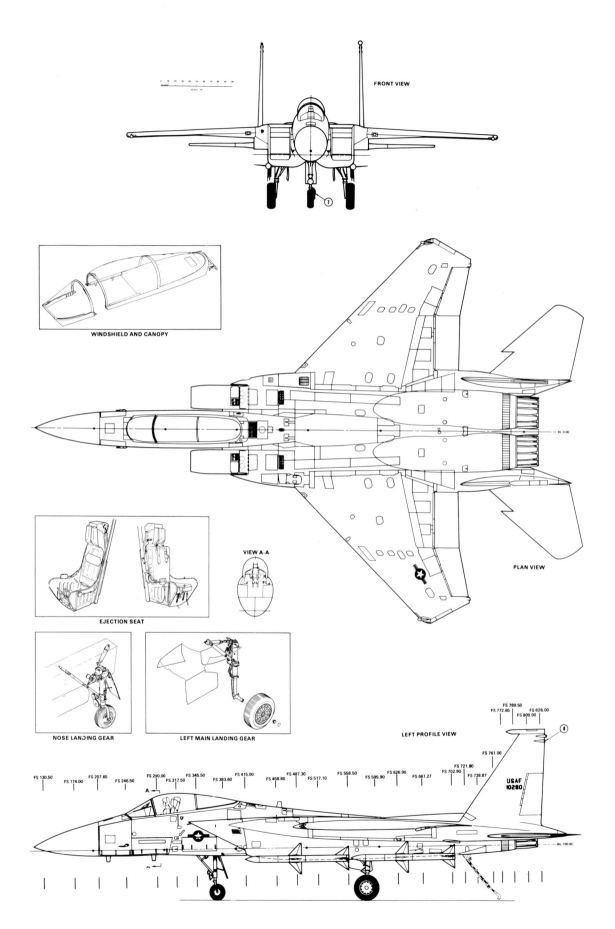

FRONT VIEW

WINDSHIELD AND CANOPY

PLAN VIEW

EJECTION SEAT

VIEW A-A

NOSE LANDING GEAR

LEFT MAIN LANDING GEAR

LEFT PROFILE VIEW

BL 0.00

WL 100.00

USAF
10280

FS 130.50   FS 207.65   FS 290.00   FS 345.50   FS 415.00   FS 487.30   FS 558.50   FS 626.90   FS 721.80
   FS 174.00   FS 246.50   FS 317.50   FS 383.60   FS 458.80   FS 517.10   FS 595.90   FS 661.27   FS 702.90   FS 738.87

FS 789.50   FS 826.00
FS 772.65   FS 809.00

FS 761.00

48

570 SQUARE FEET
OF ACCESS DOORS AND PANELS

- **SAFETY STRUTS FOR HIGH WINDS**
- **"QUICK RELEASE" ACCESS TO LRU'S**

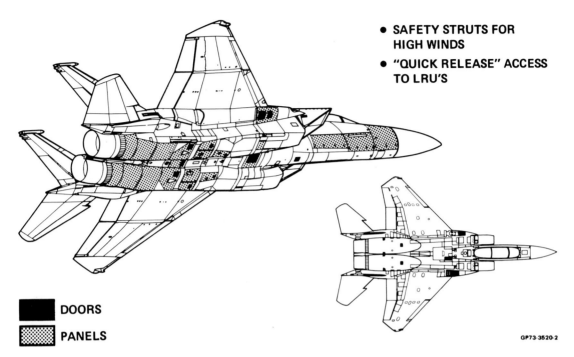

■ **DOORS**

▨ **PANELS**

GP73-3520-2

PHYSICAL CHARACTERISTICS

WING . . . .

Area (theoretical)	599.39 Sq.Ft.		
Span	42 Ft. 9.7 In.		
Aspect Ratio	3.01		
Taper Ratio	.25		
Sweep (LE)	45°		
Dihedral	-1°		
Airfoil & Chord			
Root (BL O) NACA64A006.6	$(CL_i=0)$	301.5 In. Actual	
BL 77.0 NACA64A(X)05.9	$(CL_i=.055,a=.8MOD)$	226.0 In.	
BL 155.0 NACA64A(X)04.6	$(CL_i=.055,a=.8MOD)$	149.6 In.	
BL 224.73 NACA64A203.5	$(CL_i=.20,a=.8MOD)$	94.0 In.	
Tip NACA64A203	$(CL_i=.20,a=.8MOD)$	68.3 In.	
Incidence	None		
Twist	None		
Modified Conical Camber	CL_o .3		
Aileron Area	26.48 Sq. Ft.		
Flap Area	35.84 Sq. Ft.		

HORIZONTAL STABILIZER . . . .

Area Reference L.E. Snag Provision	111.36 Sq. Ft. (55.68EA)
Area Reference Basic Geometry	120.0 Sq. Ft. (60.0EA)
Aspect Ratio	2.05
Taper Ratio	.34
Sweep (LE)	50°
Dihedral	0°
Airfoil & Chord	
Root NACA 0005.5 - 64(MOD)	137.2 In. Reference
BL 90.0 NACA 0003.5 - 64	117.9 In. Reference
Tip NACA 0002.5 - 64	46.5 In.

VERTICAL TAIL . . . .

Effective Area	125.22 Sq. Ft. (62.61EA)
Aspect Ratio	L70
Taper Ratio	.27
Sweep (LE)	36°34'
Airfoil & Chord	
Root NACA 0005 - 64	115.0 In.
Tip NACA 0003.5 - 64	30.6 In.
Rudder Area	19.94 Sq. Ft. (9.97EA)

SPEED BRAKE AREA	31.5 Sq. Ft.
CONTROL SURFACE TRAVEL	
Aileron	+ 20°
Speed Brake	45° up from ML
Rudder	+ 30°
Horizontal Stabilizer (LE)	15° Up, 26° Dn
Trailing Edge Flap	30° Down
LANDING GEAR	
Main Gear	
Tire Size	34.5x9.75-18
Stroke	9.02 In.
Static Rolling Radius	15.13 In.
Flat Rolling Radius	11.6 In.
Nose Gear	
Tire Size	22.0x6.6-10
Stroke	16.5 In.
Static Rolling Radius	9.88 In.
Flat Rolling Radius	7.0 In.
PROPULSION	(2) F100-PW-100 Engines

F/TF-15A FORWARD COCKPIT

1. NAVIGATION AIDS PANEL
2. CONTROL AUGMENTATION SYSTEM (CAS) PANEL
3. THROTTLE QUADRANT
4. EXTERIOR LIGHTS CONTROL PANEL
5. INTEGRATED COMMUNICATIONS CONTROL PANEL
6. BLANK PANEL
7. BLANK PANEL
8. ANTI-G PANEL
9. BLANK PANEL
10. BLANK PANEL
11. BLANK PANEL
12. GROUND POWER PANEL
13. BIT PANEL
14. AAI CONTROL PANEL
15. IFF CONTROL PANEL
16. TEWS CONTROL PANEL
17. RADAR CONTROL PANEL
18. BLANK PANEL
19. FUEL CONTROL PANEL
20. MISCELLANEOUS CONTROL PANEL
21. SEAT ADJUST SWITCH
22. IFF ANTENNA SELECT SWITCH
23. EMERGENCY AIR REFUELING CONTROL
24. ARMAMENT SAFETY OVERRIDE SWITCH
25. BLANK PANEL
26. V_{MAX} SWITCH

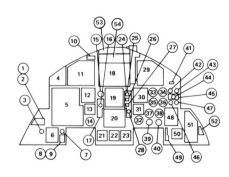

WARNING
LANDING GEAR CONTROL HANDLE MUST BE IN DOWN POSITION BEFORE OPERATING THIS SWITCH

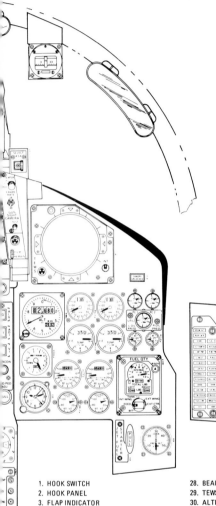

1. OXYGEN REGULATOR PANEL
2. ENVIRONMENTAL CONTROL SYSTEMS PANEL
3. CABIN TEMPERATURE CONTROL PANEL
4. CANOPY CONTROL
5. INTERIOR LIGHTS CONTROL PANEL
6. TEWS POD CONTROL PANEL
7. BLANK PANEL
8. UTILITY LIGHT
9. VACUUM BOTTLE
10. STOWAGE COMPARTMENT
11. OXYGEN/COMMUNICATIONS OUTLET PANEL
12. COMPASS CONTROL PANEL
13. TEWS CONTROL PANEL
14. NAVIGATION CONTROL PANEL
15. ENGINE CONTROL PANEL
16. ENGINE START PANEL

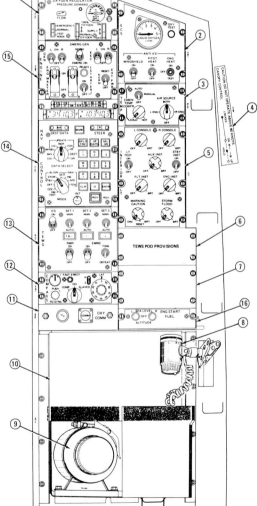

1. HOOK SWITCH
2. HOOK PANEL
3. FLAP INDICATOR
4. FIRE WARN PANEL
5. ARMT CONT'R PANEL
6. GEAR HANDLE
7. PITCH RATIO INDICATOR
8. PITCH RATIO SWITCH
9. PITCH RATIO PANEL
10. RADIO CALL PANEL
11. RADAR SCOPE
12. AIR SPEED INDICATOR
13. ANGLE OF ATTACK INDICATOR
14. G METER
15. EMER JETT SWITCH
16. STEER MODE SWITCH
17. STEER MODE PANEL
18. HUD CONTROL PANEL
19. ALTITUDE INDICATOR
20. HORIZONTAL SITUATION INDICATOR
21. AIR SPEED (STANDBY)
22. ATTITUDE (STANDBY)
23. ALTIMETER (STANDBY)
24. MASTER MODE PANEL
25. A/G MODE BUTTON
26. ADI MODE BUTTON
27. VI MODE BUTTON
28. BEACON LIGHT
29. TEWS DISPLAY
30. ALTIMETER
31. VERTICAL VELOCITY
32. CLOCK
33. LEFT TACHOMETER
34. RIGHT TACHOMETER
35. LEFT TEMPERATURE
36. RIGHT TEMPERATURE
37. LEFT FUEL FLOW
38. RIGHT FUEL FLOW
39. LEFT NOZZLE POSITION
40. RIGHT NOZZLE POSITION
41. CANOPY UNLOCKED LIGHT
42. PC1 INDICATOR
43. PC2 INDICATOR
44. UTILITY INDICATOR
45. OIL/HYD IND PANEL
46. LEFT OIL PRESS.
47. RIGHT OIL PRESS.
48. FUEL QTY INDICATOR
49. JFS PANEL
50. CABIN PRESS ALT
51. CAUTION PANEL
52. EMER VENT PANEL
53. IFF REMOTE PANEL
54. UHF REMOTE PANEL

EXTERNAL ACCESS DOORS

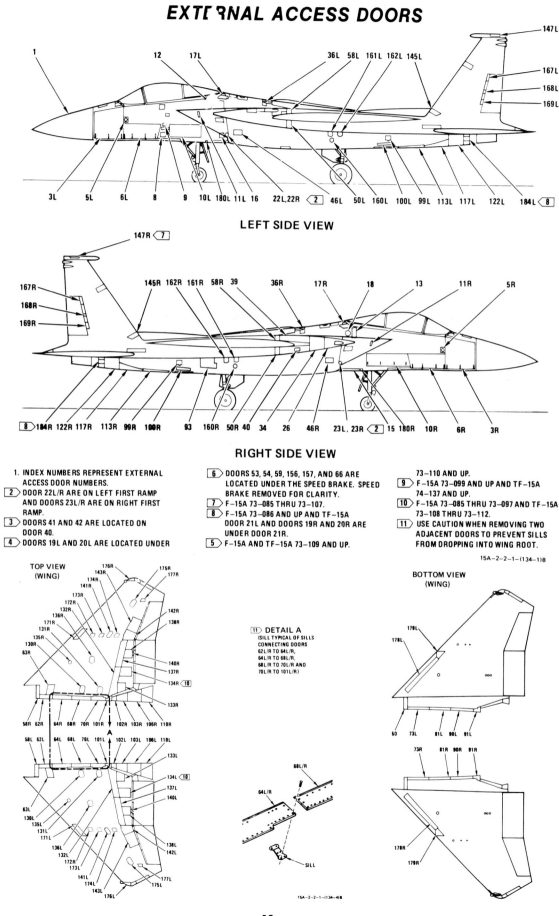

LEFT SIDE VIEW

RIGHT SIDE VIEW

1. INDEX NUMBERS REPRESENT EXTERNAL ACCESS DOOR NUMBERS.

2. DOOR 22L/R ARE ON LEFT FIRST RAMP AND DOORS 23L/R ARE ON RIGHT FIRST RAMP.

3. DOORS 41 AND 42 ARE LOCATED ON DOOR 40.

4. DOORS 19L AND 20L ARE LOCATED UNDER

5. F-15A AND TF-15A 73-109 AND UP.

6. DOORS 53, 54, 59, 156, 157, AND 66 ARE LOCATED UNDER THE SPEED BRAKE. SPEED BRAKE REMOVED FOR CLARITY.

7. F-15A 73-085 THRU 73-107.

8. F-15A 73-086 AND UP AND TF-15A DOOR 21L AND DOORS 19R AND 20R ARE UNDER DOOR 21R.

73-110 AND UP.

9. F-15A 73-099 AND UP AND TF-15A 74-137 AND UP.

10. F-15A 73-085 THRU 73-097 AND TF-15A 73-108 THRU 73-112.

11. USE CAUTION WHEN REMOVING TWO ADJACENT DOORS TO PREVENT SILLS FROM DROPPING INTO WING ROOT.

15A-2-2-1-(134-1)B

TOP VIEW (WING)

11 DETAIL A
(SILL TYPICAL OF SILLS CONNECTING DOORS 62L/R TO 64L/R, 64L/R TO 68L/R, 68L/R TO 70L/R AND 70L/R TO 101L/R)

BOTTOM VIEW (WING)

15A-2-2-1-(134-4)B

52

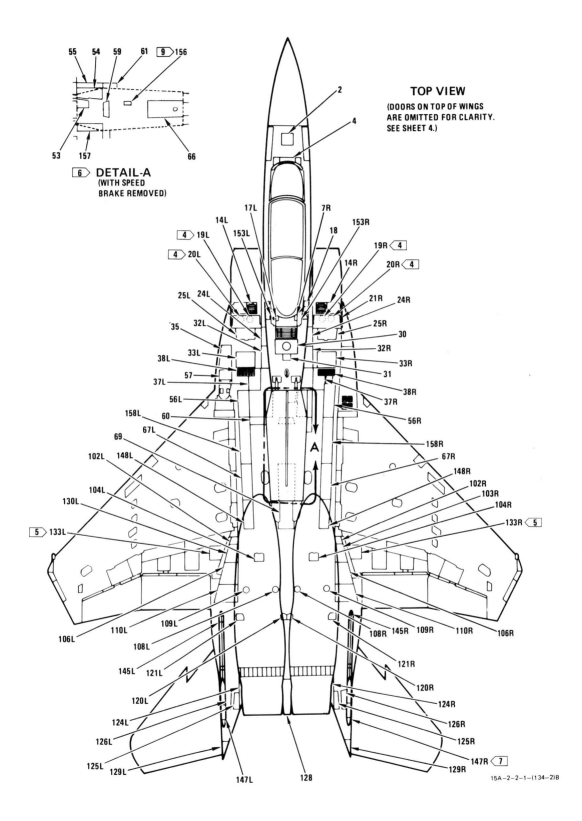

DETAIL-A
(WITH SPEED BRAKE REMOVED)

TOP VIEW
(DOORS ON TOP OF WINGS
ARE OMITTED FOR CLARITY.
SEE SHEET 4.)

15A-2-2-1-(134-2)B

53

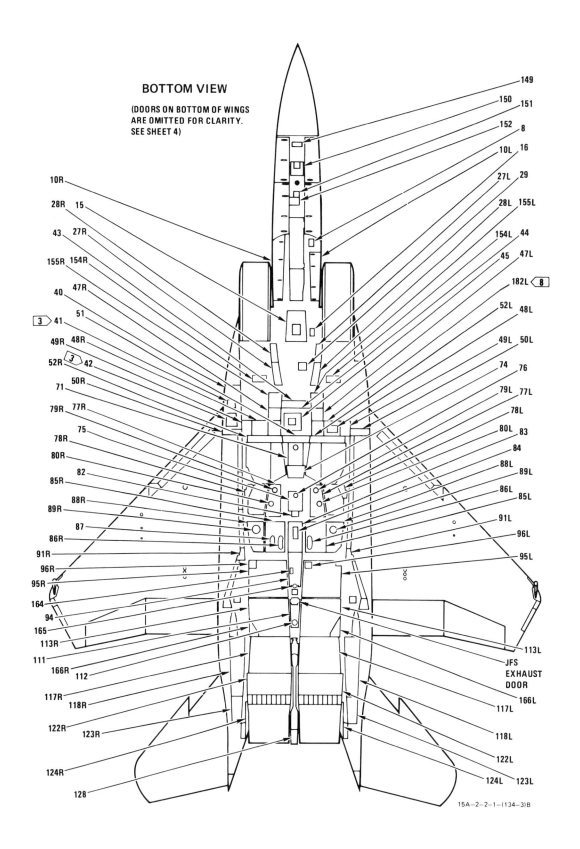

BOTTOM VIEW

(DOORS ON BOTTOM OF WINGS
ARE OMITTED FOR CLARITY.
SEE SHEET 4)

JFS
EXHAUST
DOOR

15A-2-2-1-(134-3)B

54

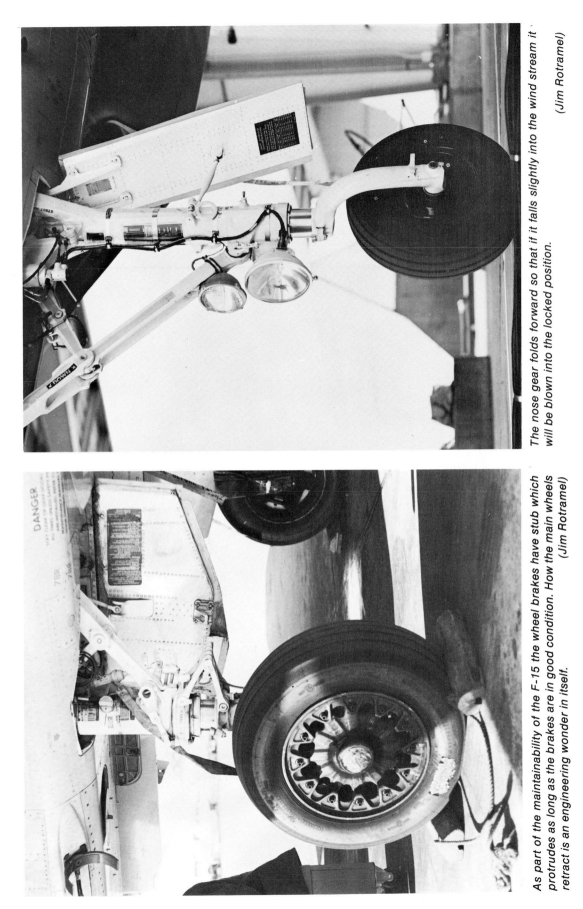

The nose gear folds forward so that if it falls slightly into the wind stream it will be blown into the locked position.
(Jim Rotramel)

As part of the maintainability of the F-15 the wheel brakes have stub which protrudes as long as the brakes are in good condition. How the main wheels retract is an engineering wonder in itself.
(Jim Rotramel)

There have been three speedbrakes: the original one on the pre-production F-15s, and the two larger ones—one with and one without the spine. The larger speedbrake with the spine was chosen for the production version.
(Jim Rotramel)

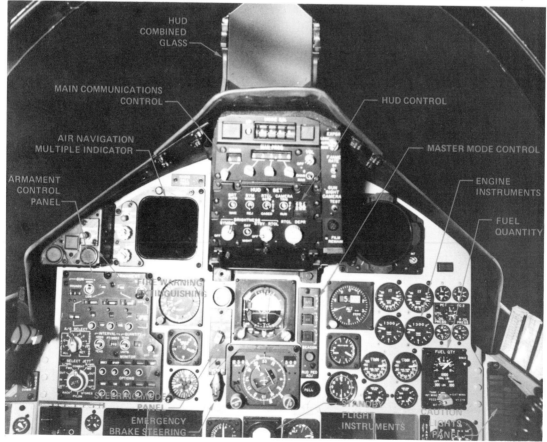

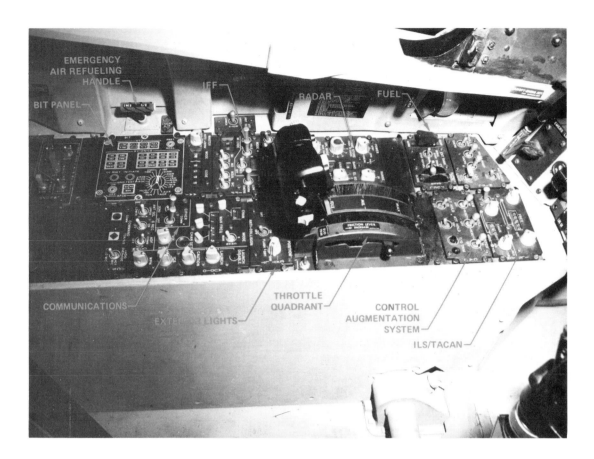

EMERGENCY
AIR REFUELING
HANDLE

BIT PANEL

IFF

RADAR

FUEL

COMMUNICATIONS

EXTERIOR LIGHTS

THROTTLE
QUADRANT

CONTROL
AUGMENTATION
SYSTEM

ILS/TACAN

ENVIRONMENTAL
CONTROL SYSTEM

INTERIOR
LIGHTS

ENGINE
CONTROL
PANEL

COMPASS
CONTROL

As a purely combat capable, dogfighting machine, there are two things that set the F-15 apart from air superiority aircraft of the past and present—the engine and the wing. The engine makes the F-15 thrust performance possible while the wing makes turning at high angles of attack possible. To really appreciate how these two work to provide the F-15 pilot the capability to outmaneuver other aircraft, a brief review of aerodynamics is helpful.

Getting back to basics, we learn that there are four forces acting on an airplane: thrust, drag, lift, and weight. The thrust of the engines must overcome the drag created by the airplane going through the air. The wing must create enough lift to overcome the pull of gravity on this mass of airplane, and this force pulling down on the aircraft we call weight. The faster the plane goes through the air, the more lift the wing will produce. When the airplane goes through the air at a constant altitude and constant speed, i.e., neither gaining nor losing altitude, and neither accelerating nor decelerating in speed, then the four forces—thrust,

words, one can look at 1 *g* as the force due to gravity in a level condition, but since the force of lift is equal to the force of gravity in a level state, a better way to look at 1 *g* is as the force due to lift. In fact, pilots talk in terms of how many *g*'s their aircraft is "pulling."

What about *g* in a turn? Anyone who has ever tied a rope to a bucket, filled it up with water, and twirled it around his head understands the concept of centrifugal force. The water does not spill out due to this centrifugal force. The bucket does not weigh any more, but it sure feels like it weighs more. In fact, the harder or faster the bucket spins around, the heavier it seems. The entire time the bucket is spinning around it does not gain mass. By speeding up or slowing down, the centrifugal force increases or decreases, but mass remains the same. The centrifugal force created by this action can be measured, and it is expressed in *g*. Therefore, if the centrifugal force is twice as much as the force of gravity the force can be expressed as 2 *g*s, and the bucket feels like it weighs twice as much.

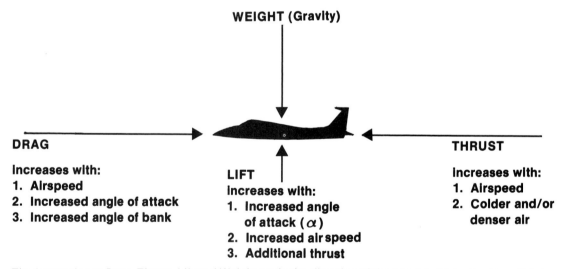

WEIGHT (Gravity)

DRAG

Increases with:
1. **Airspeed**
2. **Increased angle of attack**
3. **Increased angle of bank**

LIFT

Increases with:
1. **Increased angle of attack (α)**
2. **Increased air speed**
3. **Additional thrust**

THRUST

Increases with:
1. **Airspeed**
2. **Colder and/or denser air**

The forces due to Drag, Thrust, Lift and Weight act in the direction of the arrows. When the aircraft is in a steady state—neither gaining nor losing altitude; neither gaining nor losing airspeed—all the forces are equal. Increase any force and the opposite force must be increased to prevent a change in the steady state.

drag, lift and weight—are said to be equilibrium.

All private pilots learn that when an aircraft is banked, a force is exerted on the pilot and the force increases with the angle of bank, and is independent of aircraft type. When the plane is in level flight the pilot experiences no force other than the force of gravity which everyone feels. While the aircraft is in level flight, the force on the aircraft is said to be 1 *g*. In other

When an airplane banks, the lift from the wings has to share its forces. Not only does it have to develop a force (lift) to overcome the force due to gravity, but now it has to overcome that same force that kept the water against the bottom of the bucket—which we called centrifical force. Centrifugal force tries to make the radius of the aircraft's turn larger, especially when the airplane speeds up. Lift is defined as

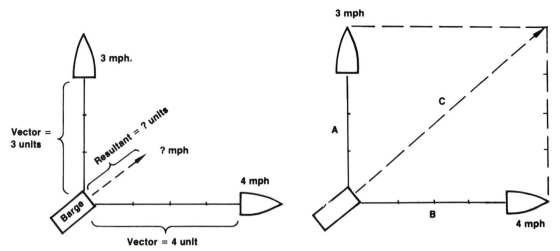

If two tug boats pull a barge—one tug boat going north and the other tug boat going east—then the barge will travel in a northeasterly direction. The speed at which it will travel (and direction) is called the "resultant" of the two "vectors" represented by the speed (and direction) of the two tug boats. Since the resultant makes the hypotenuse of a right triangle, the speed of the barge is determined by the Pythagorean formula. (See text.)

the force *perpendicular* or at right angles to the wing, but if the wing is not at right angles to the ground, how can it create lift to overcome both the weight and centrifugal force?

To understand this concept, one has only to think about two tug boats pulling a ship at 90° to each other. If each of the tug boats were pulling at the same speed, what would the ship be doing in speed? The answer is easier to understand if we give the speed of the tug boats the name vectors, and name the resulting speed of the ship, resultant.

By the use of the Pythagorean theorum that most of us learned in school, we can figure the speed of the ship, because by giving the vectors and resultants dimension with lines representing the vector's speed, the resultant becomes the hypotenuse of a right triangle. Therefore:

$$C^2 = A^2 + B^2 \quad (C^2 = 3^2 + 4^2)$$
$$C = \sqrt{A^2 + B^2} \quad (C = \sqrt{4 + 16})$$
$$C = \sqrt{25} \quad (5)$$

This same principle would work backwards as well. If the ship were doing the pulling at the speed equal to C, the tug boats would be pulled along at the same rate of speed they were previously pulling the ship.

The resultant in our example is the force of lift perpendicular to the wing, and the two vectors are the forces needed to overcome weight and centrifugal force. Now it follows that if an airplane is banked, the vector providing the lift to overcome the force of gravity is going to be less than the lift perpendicular to the wing. If the airplane was in steady flight, i.e., all the

forces in equilibrium, before banking, then the lifting force would be equal to the force due to gravity, or weight. But when the airplane banks, the lifting force now becomes a resultant—still perpendicular to the wings—which means that the vectors which are left must overcome the force of gravity and centrifugal force. If the vector left to overcome gravity is smaller than the lift created before banking, then the airplane is not getting enough lift and if nothing is done about it, it will lose altitude. The answer to this problem is that in a turn, the wing must generate even more lift than it does in level flight. In so doing, the vectors for lift and centrifugal force increase in size to overcome those two forces.

The way a wing generates more lift is by taking a bigger bite out of the air, or increasing the angle of attack. Private pilots experience this when they go into a turn because they have to pull back on the controls. Angle of attack is an important ingredient in a fighter plane because the greater the angle of attack the greater the lift until the stalling point of the wing is reached. Great amounts of time and money are spent studying the high angle of attack characteristics of a fighter aircraft because as the pilot tries to generate a tighter turn he inevitably increases the angle of attack. Airplanes have historically departed controlled flight at these high angles of attack often causing the aircraft to be lost if the pilot is unable to recover. The most common result of high angle of attack flight is a spin condition. The F-15 will spin but it is very difficult to induce and is easily recoverable.

At the beginning of this discussion on

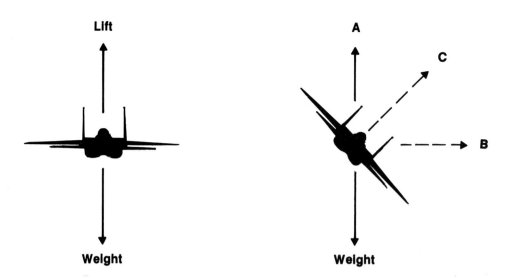

In a steady state the aircraft won't gain or lose altitude. We can represent these forces of weight and lift with lines showing their length and direction. The aircraft (above left) has a force vector of lift equal in force (length) and opposite the vector (force) due to weight. But lift is by definition, the force (vector) generated at right angles to the wings. The aircraft (above right) has banked. The force of lift generated at right angles is "C." However, to not lose altitude, the aircraft must have a "component" force due to the lift of "C" which is equal to the force due to weight or gravity. That force is "A" in the above illustration. The component "B" is the force necessary to keep the aircraft from going in a large circle or centrifugal force. By applying the solution for the hypotenuse of a right triangle "C," you can see that "C" must be larger than "A" or "B" in order to keep "A" equal to the force of weight and "B" equal to the centrifugal force.

aerodynamics we said that in a level turn, a given bank angle will produce a given g force; that if two aircraft of totally different size and configurations were at the same bank angle they would experience the same g force. Therefore, we can say that if a Cessna 150, a Boeing 747, and an F-15 were all in a 60° bank, there would be 2 g's of force on the airplane and pilot. It is also true that if two airplanes are at the same bank angle and the same airspeed, then they will have the same *radius* and *rate* of turn. Since bank angle can be expressed in g, it is safe to say that if two airplanes have the same g and airspeed they will have the same turn rate and radius. At a constant airspeed, by increasing the bank angle, the radius of turn becomes smaller and the rate of turn increases. Another way to look at these relationships is that at a constant bank angle—constant g—the faster the speed the larger the radius and the slower the rate of turn.

All this sounds like all aircraft perform the same at the same rate, radius and g, and it is true. What sets aircraft apart, then, is the ability to continue to develop lift after increasing the bank angle or g. Some wings simply stop flying after so many degrees of bank (g) or below a certain speed.

One of the major factors involved in allowing one aircraft to develop more lift in a turn than another is wing loading. Wing loading is defined as the weight of the aircraft divided by the wing area, and the lower the wing loading (pounds/square feet), the more maneuverable the aircraft. The F-15 has a wing loading down near that of the F-86 *Sabre*. The other major factor in developing a good dogfighting machine is an engine capable of giving needed thrust during these tight turns. The air that spills from under the wing, at the tip, to the lower pressure on top of the wing disrupts the airflow and degrades the lifting capability more and more the higher the angle of attack. This degradation is called induced drag because it is induced by lift itself. The only way to overcome drag is thrust, and the amount of thrust left after entering a turn is called excess thrust and is expressed as P_s or specific excess power. One of the major limiting factors in previous fighter aircraft has been the inability of the engines to put out enough thrust to compensate for the increased drag generated by the induced drag which resulted from higher angles of attack. The F-15 is the first fighter to have more thrust than weight at full takeoff combat weight. The thrust to weight ratio of the F-15 is 1.2:1 at gross takeoff combat weight and 1.4:1 at combat weight.

General Turning Performance (Constant Altitude, Steady Turn)

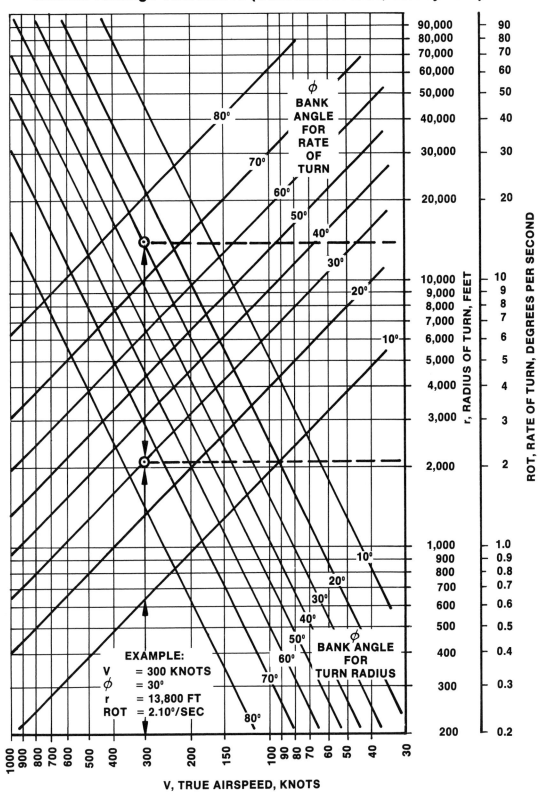

To determine the turn rate and turn radius of any aircraft, follow the example in the chart.   (U.S. Navy)

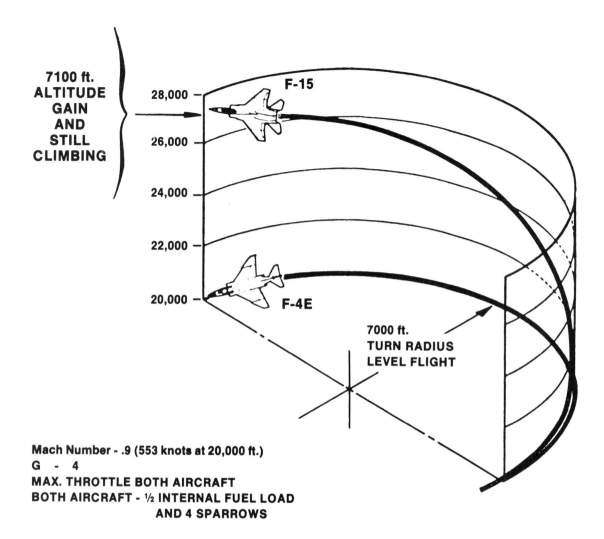

7100 ft. ALTITUDE GAIN AND STILL CLIMBING

F-15

28,000 —

26,000 —

24,000 —

22,000 —

20,000 —

F-4E

7000 ft. TURN RADIUS LEVEL FLIGHT

Mach Number - .9 (553 knots at 20,000 ft.)
G - 4
MAX. THROTTLE BOTH AIRCRAFT
BOTH AIRCRAFT - ½ INTERNAL FUEL LOAD
AND 4 SPARROWS

A good example of the superior performance of the F-15 over the F-4 Phantom. This performance bonus can be attributed to two things: The engine has enough thrust to overcome the drag induced by the increased angle of attack (α) necessary to maintain lift in the air; and secondly, the aerodynamic refinement of the wing which was designed to generate lift for the "dogfight" area, while the F-4 was designed as an interceptor. Instead of gaining altitude, the F-15 could have used excess thrust (P_S) and lifting capability of the wing to turn inside the F-4. (USAF F-15 SPO Diagram)

When the F-15 is compared to the F-4 the numbers are striking. Takeoff distance is 28 percent shorter. The acceleration time is impressive. One McDonnell Douglas pilot accelerated from .9 to 2.0 Mach in 58 seconds at 40,000 feet with a temperature of -66°C. The aircraft acceleration did not begin to taper off until it reached 1.8 Mach. This is over 100 percent faster than the F-4. Both the ceiling of 66,000 feet and the maxiumum Mach of 2.554 are higher than the F-4. The F-15 can slow down to 100 knots at 10,000 feet, increase its angle of attack to 21°, and still climb at 4,000 feet per minute.

The sustained load factor of the F-15 is 70 percent higher than the F-4. The sustained load factor is the amount of g that can be maintained in a turn. For example, at 10,000 feet the F-4 at maximum power can sustain a 5 g turn at .9 Mach while the F-15 accelerates at .9 in a 5 g turn using only military power. At .9 the F-15 sustains 6 gs again using only military power. At 30,000 feet, with both the F-4 and the F-15 in full afterburner, at 1.3 Mach, the F-4 can sustain a 3.5 g turn but the F-15 can sustain 4.8 gs. What this means in practical terms is that a 3.5 g turn gives a radius of approximately 22,000 feet while the 4.8 g turn gives a turn radius of only 14,000 feet. These same factors allow the F-15 to enter a loop at 150 knots—a figure that most military pilots do not believe.

The F100-PW-100 is a low by-pass ratio turbofan engine with a ten-stage compressor pressure ratio of 8:1 and an overall pressure ratio of 23:1. The F100 engine comes apart in 5 different components so keeping track of the engine time is more difficult than on an engine that stays in one piece. A V_{max} switch just to the left of the throttle (No. 26 on the cockpit diagram) increases the thrust approximately 2500 pounds per engine so that the F-15 can develop close to 55,000 pounds of thrust. The V_{max} switch can be used up to three hours between engine overhauls. (McDonnell Douglas)

F100-PW-100 Engine

The F100-PW-100 engine—commonly called the F100—is built by Pratt & Whitney. It is this engine (coupled with the airplane's efficient aerodynamic design) that has allowed the F-15 to set the climb to altitude records, ignore high induced drag, and fight in the vertical plane. There are aircraft designers that believe that the history of develpment of fighter aircraft can be directly tied with the development of aircraft engines. This has never been truer than with the F-15.

The F100 evolved from a competition with General Electric who submitted their model GE1/10 in the ATEGG (Advanced Turbine Engine Gas Generator) program. The original Request for Proposal (RFP) was issued in April 1968, with Pratt & Whitney announced as the winner on February 27, 1970. The F100 has its roots in three production engines: the TF30-P-1 designed for the F-111; the TF30-P-412 used in the F-14A; and the J58 used for the SR-71.

Even though the Air Force and Navy got away from the common aircraft concept with the F-111A and F-111B there still remained the idea of sharing the technological costs on the development of the advanced technology engine that was to drive the F-15. The Navy wanted a more powerful engine to power the F-14B and indeed, the F-14 was originally scheduled to get the advanced engine after the first 32 F-14A's were delivered. Pratt & Whitney responded to the RFP with the idea of building a common core gas generator, but varying the size of the fans, fan ducts, and afterburner to develop the greater thrust for the Navy engine which they called the F401-PW-400.

The Joint Engine Project Office (JEPO) was responsible to both program directors. The F-15 SPO had primary management responsibility.

The Navy hoped that the F401 engine would be developed in time to be used in the F-14's that were scheduled for deployment in 1973. The Navy ran into funding problems. Since they had an airplane with an engine, when they were pressed for money they looked around and took it from the F401 pot. Consequently, the Navy notified the Air Force in July 1971 that it would not pick up its option for the F401's.

The F100 engine endurance qualification test is the only milestone that the F-15 failed to meet on time. The F100 was supposed to meet a 150 hour milestone which involved running for 150 hours at various simulated altitudes and Mach numbers. In February 1973, seven

ADVANCED TECHNOLOGY ENGINE

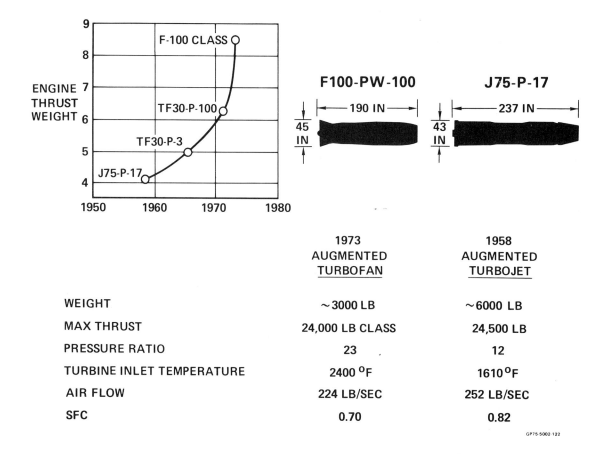

	F100-PW-100	J75-P-17
	1973 AUGMENTED TURBOFAN	1958 AUGMENTED TURBOJET
WEIGHT	~3000 LB	~6000 LB
MAX THRUST	24,000 LB CLASS	24,500 LB
PRESSURE RATIO	23	12
TURBINE INLET TEMPERATURE	2400 °F	1610 °F
AIR FLOW	224 LB/SEC	252 LB/SEC
SFC	0.70	0.82

GP75-5002-122

months after the F-15 had made its first flight on July 27, 1972, the engine failed a fan and turbine blade. Since the allocation of money was a function of meeting milestones the Department of Defense approved the first production F100's on condition that the F100 meet its 150 hour milestone by May 1973. The Air Force was desperate to reach the modified milestone schedule for two reasons. They had hung their hats on this advanced technology engine which had never flown in an aircraft before the F-15's first flight. Secondly, they had had an unblemished development with the F-15 and did not want this to bring back the haunting ghost of their two previous failures—the C-5A and the F-111. In an attempt to meet the May deadline, General Bellis modified two parts of the endurance test—the very high Mach, and high altitude portions—to ensure an on-time completion and subsequent production decision. Rather than slow the development, which would be costly and delay the program,

General Bellis made the decision—well within his authority—to modify the test points because he knew pressure on the fan could cause bending and possible failure. Instead of praise for his business-like decision, his decision was interpreted as a subterfuge. It was a public affairs problem more than a technical one.

It was this specific problem that led to the appointment of a public affairs officer—Major Broening—to advise the F-15 System Program Director General Bellis, and to expedite release of accurate information. The fault turned out to be in the test chamber walls themselves. The walls had rust on them, and when this rust contaminated the test engine, it had caused the failure.

An *ad hoc* committee of independent experts were requested by the SPO to verify the rust problem. The F100 engine produced so much thrust, it rattled the test chamber, causing the rust to flake off and be ingested into the engine at subsonic speeds. The rust coated

From left to right are McDonnell Chief Experimental Test Pilot Pete Garrison, who did the preliminary work-up on the Streak Eagle project; Major Willard "Mac" MacFarlane, who set the 6-, 9-, and 12-thousand meter records in one flight; Major Roger Smith who set the 3-, 20-, and 30-thousand meter altitude records; and Major David Peterson who flew the 15- and 25-thousand meter record setting flights.   *(McDonnell Douglas)*

the blades which affected their cooling and aerodynamic capabilities. Once this cause had been discovered, the new test program delivered a successful F100 engine on October 12, 1973.

Streak Eagle

The F100 engine's low weight and high thrust contribute to the overall high thrust to weight ratio which allowed the F-15 to set 8 world altitude records between January 16 and February 1, 1975 in operation *Streak Eagle.*

The aircraft destined to make aviation history was the 19th pre-production aircraft, F-17. The *Streak Eagle* F-15 had unnecessary weight removed, which included the missiles, radar, M-61 cannon, tail hook, one of the generators and the utility hydraulic system, flap, and speed brake actuators. In addition, the decision not to paint F-17 saved about 40 pounds. However, additional weight required for the specific mission was put back into the *Streak Eagle* aircraft. A holdback device was substituted in place of the tail hook; special battery

packs and controls were added because of the inevitable flameout above 80,000 feet; and the noseboom with alpha and beta vanes was added to determine angle of attack and slideslip respectively. The record attempt required an over the shoulder camera, sensitive *g* meter, battery powered radio, standby attitude gyro, and equipment to verify the altitudes achieved. The plane also needed ballast. All of this resulted in the empty *Streak Eagle* F-17 weighing about 2,800 pounds less than production aircraft. Only enough fuel was carried to fly each profile and return to the airfield. The weight of fuel varied from 3,000 to 6,000 pounds.

The beginning development of a possible *Streak Eagle* flight began back in 1973. The high thrust to weight made the F-15 a natural to attempt to break the time to altitude record. The computers gave the McDonnell Douglas engineers readings that indicated that the F-15 could easily break the records of the F-4 and the MiG-25 *Foxbat.*

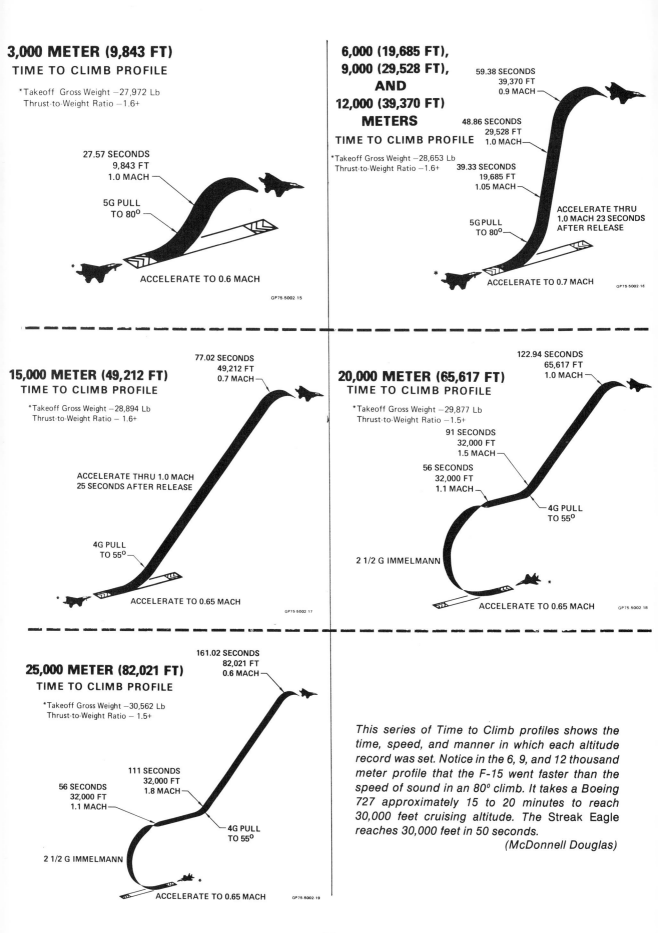

3,000 METER (9,843 FT)
TIME TO CLIMB PROFILE

*Takeoff Gross Weight —27,972 Lb
Thrust-to-Weight Ratio —1.6+

27.57 SECONDS
9,843 FT
1.0 MACH

5G PULL
TO 80°

ACCELERATE TO 0.6 MACH

GP75-5002-15

6,000 (19,685 FT),
9,000 (29,528 FT),
AND
12,000 (39,370 FT)
METERS
TIME TO CLIMB PROFILE

*Takeoff Gross Weight —28,653 Lb
Thrust-to-Weight Ratio —1.6+

59.38 SECONDS
39,370 FT
0.9 MACH

48.86 SECONDS
29,528 FT
1.0 MACH

39.33 SECONDS
19,685 FT
1.05 MACH

ACCELERATE THRU
1.0 MACH 23 SECONDS
AFTER RELEASE

5G PULL
TO 80°

ACCELERATE TO 0.7 MACH

GP75-5002-16

15,000 METER (49,212 FT)
TIME TO CLIMB PROFILE

*Takeoff Gross Weight —28,894 Lb
Thrust-to-Weight Ratio — 1.6+

77.02 SECONDS
49,212 FT
0.7 MACH

ACCELERATE THRU 1.0 MACH
25 SECONDS AFTER RELEASE

4G PULL
TO 55°

ACCELERATE TO 0.65 MACH

GP75-5002-17

20,000 METER (65,617 FT)
TIME TO CLIMB PROFILE

*Takeoff Gross Weight —29,877 Lb
Thrust-to-Weight Ratio —1.5+

122.94 SECONDS
65,617 FT
1.0 MACH

91 SECONDS
32,000 FT
1.5 MACH

56 SECONDS
32,000 FT
1.1 MACH

4G PULL
TO 55°

2 1/2 G IMMELMANN

ACCELERATE TO 0.65 MACH

GP75-5002-18

25,000 METER (82,021 FT)
TIME TO CLIMB PROFILE

*Takeoff Gross Weight —30,562 Lb
Thrust-to-Weight Ratio —1.5+

161.02 SECONDS
82,021 FT
0.6 MACH

111 SECONDS
32,000 FT
1.8 MACH

56 SECONDS
32,000 FT
1.1 MACH

4G PULL
TO 55°

2 1/2 G IMMELMANN

ACCELERATE TO 0.65 MACH

GP75-5002-19

This series of Time to Climb profiles shows the time, speed, and manner in which each altitude record was set. Notice in the 6, 9, and 12 thousand meter profile that the F-15 went faster than the speed of sound in an 80° climb. It takes a Boeing 727 approximately 15 to 20 minutes to reach 30,000 feet cruising altitude. The Streak Eagle reaches 30,000 feet in 50 seconds.

(McDonnell Douglas)

30,000 METER (98,425 FT)
TIME TO CLIMB PROFILE

*Takeoff Gross Weight —31,908 Lb
Thrust-to-Weight Ratio — 1.4+

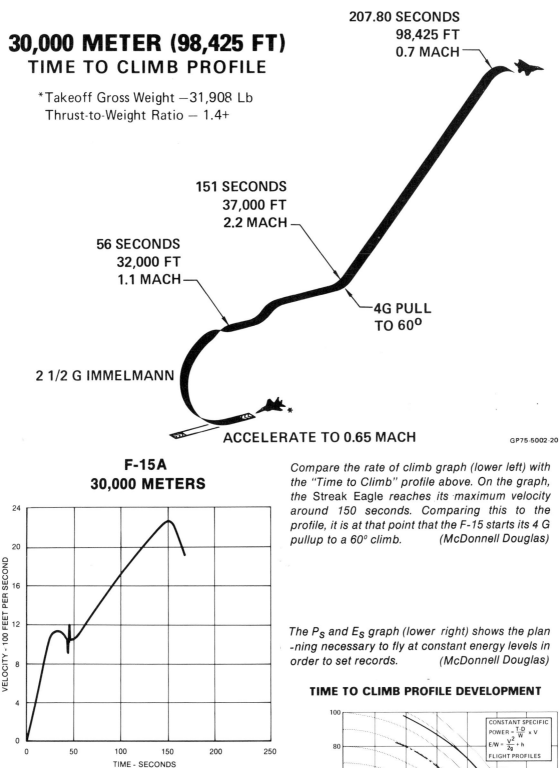

**207.80 SECONDS
98,425 FT
0.7 MACH**

**151 SECONDS
37,000 FT
2.2 MACH**

**4G PULL
TO 60°**

**56 SECONDS
32,000 FT
1.1 MACH**

2 1/2 G IMMELMANN

ACCELERATE TO 0.65 MACH

GP75-5002-20

F-15A
30,000 METERS

VELOCITY - 100 FEET PER SECOND

TIME - SECONDS

This graph shows the rate of climb in feet per second for McAir F-17, the Streak Eagle record setting aircraft. To convert from feet/second to feet/minute multiply ft/sec x 60. = ft/minute. To convert from feet/second to miles per hour, multiply the feet/second by 0.68.
Example: 660 ft/sec x 60 = 39,000 ft/min.
660 ft/sec x 0.68 = 449 miles/hour

Compare the rate of climb graph (lower left) with the "Time to Climb" profile above. On the graph, the Streak Eagle *reaches its maximum velocity around 150 seconds. Comparing this to the profile, it is at that point that the F-15 starts its 4 G pullup to a 60° climb.* (McDonnell Douglas)

The P_S and E_S graph (lower right) shows the planning necessary to fly at constant energy levels in order to set records. (McDonnell Douglas)

TIME TO CLIMB PROFILE DEVELOPMENT

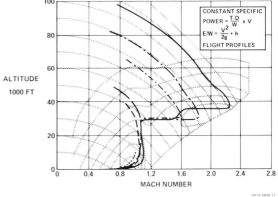

ALTITUDE
1000 FT

MACH NUMBER

CONSTANT SPECIFIC
POWER = $\frac{T-D}{W}$ x V
E/W = $\frac{V^2}{2g}$ + h
FLIGHT PROFILES

GP75 5032 11

F-15 SMASHES FOXBAT CLIMB MARKS!

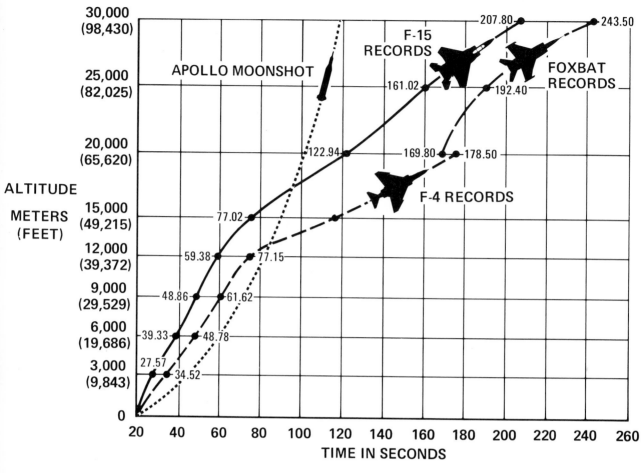

Imagine an astronaut's surprise if he were to watch an F-15 outclimb him to almost 60,000 feet. This chart is not up-to-date as the MiG-25 Foxbat has recaptured some of the higher altitude records.

(McDonnell Douglas)

GP75-5158-1

The records set are now history and well documented. What is not well known is the story behind the Russian attempt to take away the climb to altitude records to 25,000 and 30,000 feet. On May 17, 1975 the Russians allegedly flew to those altitudes, broke the F-15 records, and set a new record to 35,000 feet. The evidence sent to the National Aeronautic Administration (NAA), the American representative of the FAI who validates attempts, is unconvincing. Part of the FAI rules call for make and type of aircraft, brief description, and identification marks. Here is what the NAA received from the Russians:

(1) Make (Designation): E-266M
(2) Type: Airplane with reaction engines.

(3) Brief description: Entirely metallic monoplane with two turbojet engines.
(4) Identification marks: Flight number 601, red stars on the wings and on the vertical tail.

There was little supporting proof to back up the claims of the Russians, and what was sent when subjected to analysis appeared to indicate that the E-266M (which is a modified MiG-25) was rocket assisted. The acceleration curves, the engineers claimed were capable only by this rocket assistance. The Soviet reply to the challenge was basically that gentlemen do not question gentlemen.

The Soviets have since sent additional data on their record attempts and their records were validated by the FAI on January 1, 1977

One of the few photos to show the air-superiority role of the F-15. This air-superiority blue F-15 has 4 AIM-9L Sidewinder *and 4 AIM-7F* Sparrow *missiles mounted underneath.*

The Streak Eagle *aircraft 72-0119 was about ten percent lighter than the production aircraft. It climbed to almost 100,000 feet in the time you could soft-boil an egg. The design "Aquila Maxima" was taken off before the actual flight.*
(McDonnell Douglas)

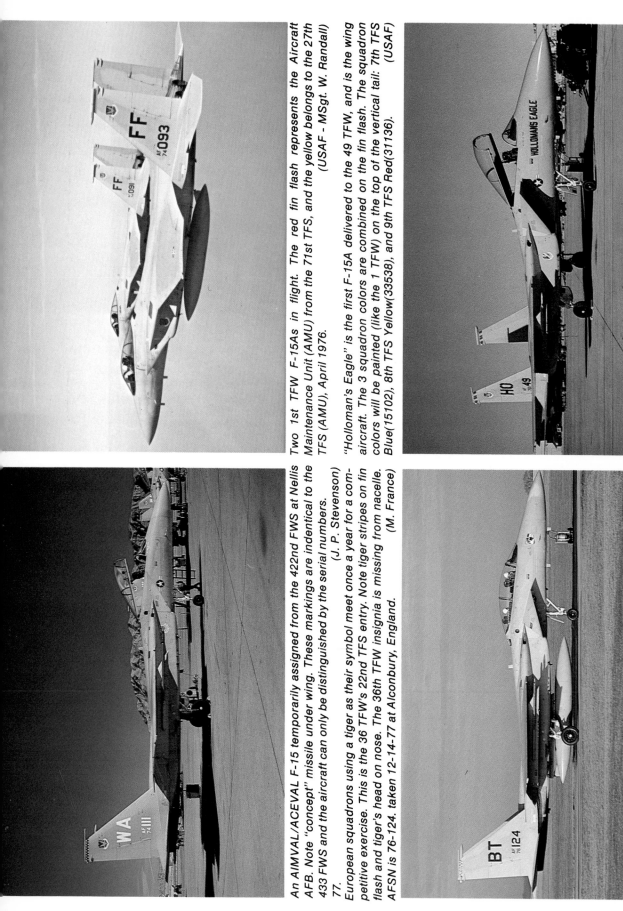

An AIMVAL/ACEVAL F-15 temporarily assigned from the 422nd FWS at Nellis AFB. Note "concept" missile under wing. These markings are identical to the 433 FWS and the aircraft can only be distinguished by the serial numbers. (J. P. Stevenson)

European squadrons using a tiger as their symbol meet once a year for a competitive exercise. This is the 36 TFW's 22nd TFS entry. Note tiger stripes on fin flash and tiger's head on nose. The 36th TFW insignia is missing from nacelle. AFSN is 76-124. taken 12-14-77 at Alconbury, England. (M. France)

Two 1st TFW F-15As in flight. The red fin flash represents the Aircraft Maintenance Unit (AMU) from the 71st TFS, and the yellow belongs to the 27th TFS (AMU), April 1976. (USAF - MSgt. W. Randall)

"Holloman's Eagle" is the first F-15A delivered to the 49 TFW, and is the wing aircraft. The 3 squadron colors are combined on the fin flash. The squadron colors will be painted (like the 1 TFW) on the top of the vertical tail: 7th TFS Blue(15102), 8th TFS Yellow(33538), and 9th TFS Red(31136). (USAF)

70

An artist's rendering of F-15s in Thunderbird paint scheme. (McDonnell Douglas)

AF Serial No. 71-291 (TF-2) in Bicentennial paint scheme. This same scheme flew across the Pacific with the Bicentennial Star replaced by a globe.
(McDonnell Douglas)

Capt. Gerald B. Fleming USAF pilots a TF-15A (F-15B)AFSN 74-0139 in Ferris paint scheme with author in back seat. Photo taken with 15mm lens with 170° diagonal field of view. Wing tips are distorted to appear as horizontal tail, 8-17-76.
(J. P. Stevenson)

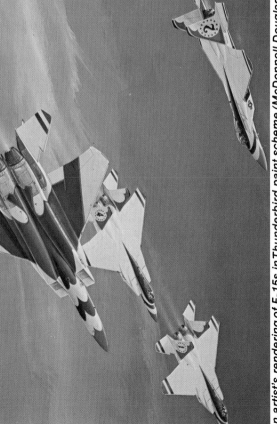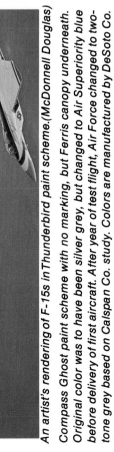

Compass Ghost paint scheme with no marking, but Ferris canopy underneath. Original color was to have been silver grey, but changed to Air Superiority blue before delivery of first aircraft. After year of test flight, Air Force changed to two-tone grey based on Calspan Co. study. Colors are manufactured by DeSoto Co. Compass Ghost first used on 34th single seat, and 10th two-seat F-15. This is AFSN 74-0113 of the 461 TFTS.
(Jim Rotramel)

71

MATERIAL DISTRIBUTION

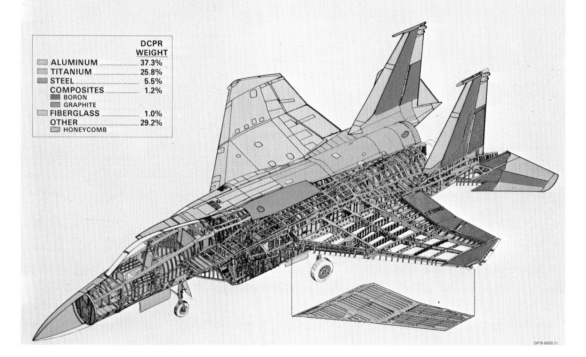

	DCPR WEIGHT
ALUMINUM	37.3%
TITANIUM	25.8%
STEEL	5.5%
COMPOSITES	1.2%
BORON	
GRAPHITE	
FIBERGLASS	1.0%
OTHER	29.2%
HONEYCOMB	

QP76-6000-31

The Keith Ferris attitude-deception paint scheme on AFSN 74-0139.   *(Keith Ferris)*

The 36-inch planar radar sits in front of the continuous wave antenna located near the top. Notice the convenience of the "black boxes" which are located in reach of ground maintenance personnel.

(McDonnell Douglas)

Avionics and Weapons System

The F-15 was unique in development in that the avionics and weapons system were totally integrated. The contractor was responsible for the bringing together of all the different subsystems to create an orchestrated group that makes—with the exception of several small analog interfacing processors—the F-15 the first all digital aircraft.

The avionics systems make up the aviation electronics that does everything from tell the aircraft where it has been to where it wants the weapons to go. The Fire Control System which is commonly thought of as the radar, searches out targets, and once they are acquired the radar locks on to the targets to provide the necessary guidance for the AIM-7F *Sparrow*

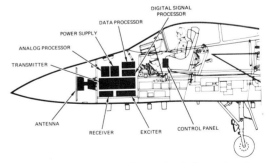

missile, or seeker head manipulations for the AIM-9L *Sidewinder* infrared missile, or for guidance in gun tracking. The fire control indicators give the pilot the information on the digitally process screen or on the Head Up Display (HUD). These two instruments are used in the navigation to a ground attack target

F-15 AVIONICS SIMPLIFIED BLOCK DIAGRAM

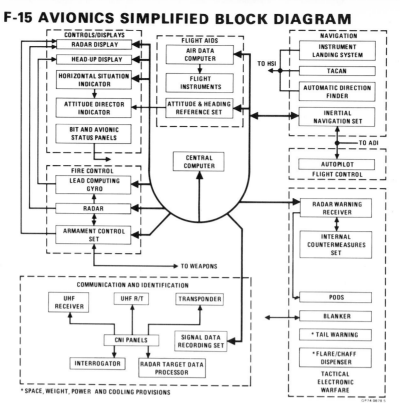

One of the advantages of digital computers is that they allow all of the different instruments to talk to each other. This ability expands the capability of the F-15 and saves space. How they talk to each other is shown in this illustration.

(McDonnell Douglas)

as well as for computation to deliver ordnance.

The Weapon Delivery System is responsible for the selection, monitoring, and firing of the selected weapon. The mountings that carry these weapons are also part of this system.

Radio Navigation provides the pilot with a back up to the inertial navigation system in the form of an attitude, heading reference system, and ILS landing system. The UHF communication system gives the pilot either a normal or secure communication capability.

The instruments are considered a subsystem within themselves. They can talk to each other by way of the Central Computer, exchange information, and keep each other updated. The instruments are all digital. The IFF (Identification Friend or Foe) system can challenge a target on the radar screen to identify whether it is friendly or not. The F-15 can, through the IFF system, identify ground targets too.

The Tactical Electronic Warfare System (TEWS) is an internally integrated electronic counter measure system which can detect an enemy threat and provide a method to defeat the electronic threat. The TEWS is composed of a radar warning receiver, tail warning set, interference blanker, internal countermeasures set, and flare/chaff dispenser.

To monitor all these systems the F-15 has another system known as the Built in Test (BIT). This system monitors the various avionic systems, and when there is a failure, isolates the area so that the pilot can tell the maintenance personnel the source of the problem. The BIT system is implemented by Line Replaceable Units (LRU). Most of the black boxes are located in the nose. The crew chiefs can scan the individual units of black boxes, and where there has been a failure, a white three-sided figure will appear. The LRU can be taken out and replaced immediately, allowing the F-15 a quick turnaround and the black box can be fixed back at the avionics shop.

The heart of the avionics systems is the IBM CP-1075/AYK Central Computer. The computer does the computations for the Heads Up Display, navigation, weapons delivery and control, and display systems. For the computer buff, the computer has 16,384—34 bit—words which is expandable to 24,576 words. It is capable of performing 340,000 instructions per second.

The F-15 used at the AIMVAL/ACEVAL test at Nellis AFB in Nevada took out the air to ground capability in its radar computer (081 box) in order to use part of the computer for some special tests during the 10-month test period. These AIMVAL/ACEVAL innovations and improvements are supposed to be modifications that will be incorporated into the production and squadron aircraft.

There are many smaller computers that make up the avionics and weapons system on the F-15. Of these, the Air Data Computer is the most significant. This computer takes information from the pilot static system, angle of attack sensor, and the total temperature probe. It gives information back to the two altimeters, angle of attack indicator, two airspeed indicators, and the vertical speed indicator. The Air Data Computer shares this information with the Automatic Flight Control Set, lead computing gyro, IFF transponder, and, of course, the Central Computer. Most of the other subsystems give information to their corresponding instruments directly and by way of the Central Computer.

VI MODE STEERING

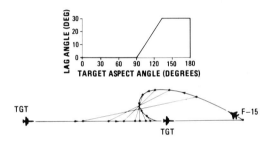

By pressing a button, the computer and radar can position an F-15 to the rear and slightly below the target. *(McDonnell Douglas)*

The Fire Control Radar commands the most attention of all the avionics systems because it is the focal point of what the F-15 is all about. The F-15 weapons system differs from the F-14 in that the Airborne Weapons Group 9 (AWG-9) was developed by Hughes Aircraft Company for the government with existing off-the-shelf components (GFE) to be furnished by the government to Grumman to integrate into the F-14. McDonnell Douglas, on the other hand, asked for the responsibility to make the weapons systems contractor furnish equipment (CFE) and to integrate those subcontractors avionic products that they felt would provide the best product and service.

The Fire Control Radar Set AN/APG-63 (or -64 if it has the Continuous Wave illumination built into the radar set) is a coherent X-band multiple Pulse Repetition Frequency (PRF) radar with a 36-inch planar array with L-band IFF antenna. The radar information is displayed on either the radar screen (also called the Multiple Air Navigation Indicator [MANI] because of its other navigation and electro-optical uses) or on the Head Up Display.

Throughout the development of the F-15, the Air Force constantly recited the litany: "Not a pound for Air-to-Ground." They wanted to make it clear that this aircraft would be designed for the air-to-air role and any air-to-ground capability would be a fallout. However, in addition to the air-to-air capability of the radar system, the F-15 has an excellent air-to-ground capability.

The master modes of the F-15 weapons system are Air-to-Air, Air-to-Ground (A/G), Attitude Director Indicator (ADI), and Visual Identification (VI). Whenever the last three are not selected, the F-15 is in the Air-to-Air mode.

The Air-to-Ground mode speaks for itself. When this button is pushed, which is located right of the attitude indicator, all of the computers and avionic systems are tensed up for an air-to-ground ordnance delivery. The ADI is the navigation mode and puts navigation data on the Head Up Display (HUD). However, by selecting the ADI, the attack displays on the radar screen are not destroyed and the ability to fire the gun or launch missiles is maintained. The pilot selects the VI mode when he wants to make a visual identification of a target. This mode gives steering commands to the pilot that tell him to steer a dot into a circle—much like a flight director—which will position him behind, below, and slightly to the right of the target.

Air-to-Air

In the air-to-air operation the radar provides target range, range rate, as well as azimuth, elevation, angle, and rates. The radar has azimuth scan patterns of 20, 60, and 120 degrees; elevation scan patterns of 1, 2, 4, 6 and 8 bars; and range selection of 10, 20, 40, 80, and 160 miles.

The mode selection knob on the radar control panel just to the left of the throttles allows the pilot to select the major modes of the radar system. The longest range available on the radar is Velocity Search (VS). The radar transmits high PRF waveforms only and can only search in this mode. Target information is in range rate and azimuth only. The closure or opening rate of the target must be greater than that of the F-15, and therefore only closing or opening targets can be detected. Ranges are available out to 160 miles and greater.

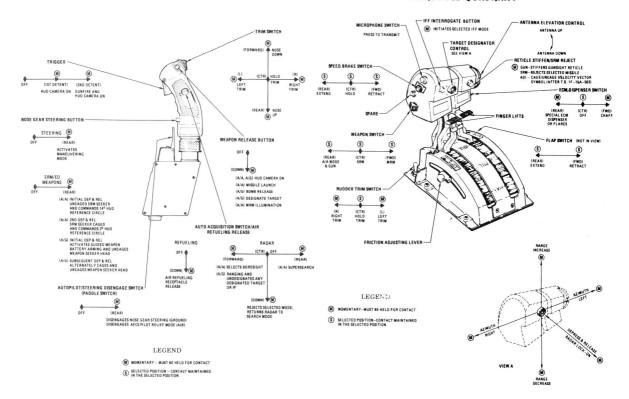

A summary of the F-15 Weapons system capability.

MISSION	RADAR	MAN or AUTO	MODE	PULSE (PRF) REPETITION FREQUENCY	SEARCH or TRACK	PRIME FUNCTION	WEAPONS CAPABILITY	ANTENNA PROGRAM	NOMINAL DETECTION RANGE	DISPLAY FORMAT
Air to Air	Pulse Doppler	Manual	Velocity Search (VS)	High	Search	Long range detection on closing targets.	Detection only.	20°, 60°, 120° AZ 1, 2, 4, 6, 8 Bar	120-160 NM	Velocity v. Azimuth
			Long Range Search (LRS)	High and Medium	Search	Long range detection and acquisition.		Same as (VS)	100 NM	Range v. Azimuth (B Scan)
					Track Track					**TARGET DATA** True air speed, aspect angle Altitude, range, range rate
			Short Range Search (SRS)	Medium	Search/Track	Detection and acquisition 10 miles or less.	AIM-9L Gun	Same as (VS)	10 NM	
	Pulse		Pulse	Low	Search/Track	Air to air backup to all radar modes except supersearch.		Same as (VS)		Range v. Azimuth
		Manual and/or Automatic	Manual Track			Backup Angle Tracking.		3° azimuth 2 Bar Scan		
			Flood	High				16° azimuth 40° elevation (Gimbled antenna lockdown in 60° position).	2 NM	
	Pulse Doppler	Automatic	Search			Automatically selects type of Radar and antenna pattern best suited for weapon selected.	Gun	HUD Field of View 20° az 20° elev	10 NM	
							AIM-9L	120° 2 bar	20 NM	
							AIM-7F	120° az 4 bar	8 NM	
			Supersearch	Medium		Automatic acquisition of target within HUD Field of View.		HUD Field of View 20° 6 bar	10 NM	
			Boresight	Medium		Automatic target acquisition along aircraft boresight line.				
			Visual Ident (VI)			Gives commands after lockon to steer behind, below slightly to right for visual ID.				
Air to Air or Air to Ground		Manual and/or Automatic	Beacon			Interrogation of beacon transponder.				B Scan format air to air and Plan Position Indicator in air to ground.
			Sniff			Passive/active radar to detect noise jamming (X-band passive).	none			
Air to Ground			Doppler (DRLR)			Navigational Update function.	none	90° az 15° down		No display
			Ranging (RNG)			Slant range measurements.				10 NM Plan Position Indicator
	Pulse		Ground Map					100° + 10° 1 bar		Plan Position Indicator of ground returns

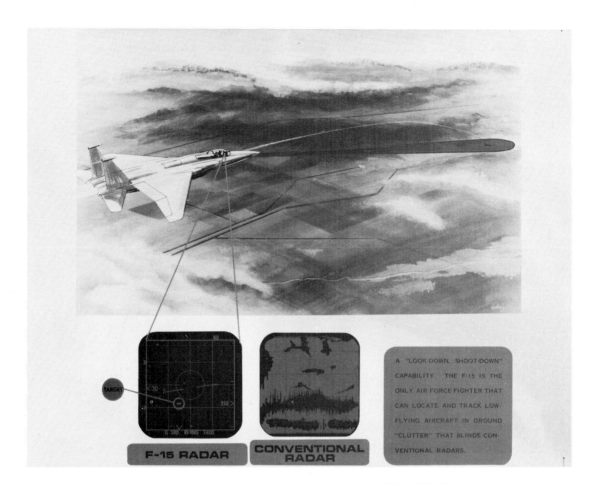

F-15 RADAR CONVENTIONAL RADAR

A "LOOK DOWN, SHOOT-DOWN" CAPABILITY. THE F-15 IS THE ONLY AIR FORCE FIGHTER THAT CAN LOCATE AND TRACK LOW-FLYING AIRCRAFT IN GROUND "CLUTTER" THAT BLINDS CONVENTIONAL RADARS.

The next longest mode is Long Range Search (LRS). This is the basic air-to-air mode because of its multiple capabilities. Any bar scan pattern can be used, as well as any range selection. While the radar is searching in high PRF the display gives angle and velocity information, but once it begins to track, the radar gives angle, velocity and range. The radar switches between high and medium PRF in the LRS mode. Where a target is beyond the medium PRF range, the radar uses FM ranging on the high PRF waveform every ½ second, with burst of medium PRF every 3 seconds to try to recapture a lost target, or find a new one. After acquisition, the VSD (Vertical Situation Display) or ANMI gives true airspeed, maneuvering *g*, aspect angle, altitude, range, and range rate, which is the opening or closing velocity.

Air-to-Ground

Even though the Air Force claimed that they would not spend a pound for air-to-ground, the axiom that a good air-to-air machine can end up as a good air-to-ground aircraft—but not vice versa—seems especially true in the F-15's

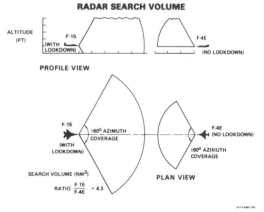

RADAR SEARCH VOLUME

This schematic showing the various distances and volumes of the radar coverage of the F-15 and the F-4 shows the significant increase associated with the F-15. (McDonnell Douglas)

case. It is also true that the F-15 was designed from the beginning to have air-to-ground capability in spite of the comments to the contrary.

There are three air-to-ground radar modes that are initiated by selecting A/G on the master mode panel. The doppler mode provides navigational updates by positioning the anten-

EXTERNAL STORES LOADING

STORES	WEIGHT (LB)	9	8	7	6	5	4	3	2	1	TOTAL	ENVELOPE SPEED	"G"
AIR-TO-AIR MISSILES												FULL A/C ENVELOPE	
● AIM-7F	510			1	1		1	1			4		
● AIM-9E/L	168/199		2						2		4/4		
GENERAL PURPOSE/DEMOLITION BOMBS												700 KCAS M = 1.4	−3 TO +7.33
● MK-82 SLICK	505		6			6			6		18		
● MK-82 SNAKEYE	560		6			6			6		18		
● MK-84 SLICK	1970		1			1			1		3		
FIRE BOMBS		ECM PODS								ECM PODS		600 KCAS M = 0.95	−2 TO +6
● BLU-27B/B (FINNED AND UNFINNED)	814/799		3			3			3		9/9		
GUIDED BOMBS												650 KCAS M = 1.2	
● MK-84 LASER	2053		1			1			1		3		−2 TO +5
● MK-84 EO	2276		1			1			1		3	550 KCAS M = 0.95	
● MK-84 IR	2123		1			1			1		3		
DISPENSERS												700 KCAS M = 1.4	−2 TO +6
● CBU-52B/B	785		4			4			4		12		
● CBU-58/B	820		4			4			4		12		
● CBU-71/B	820		4			4			4		12		
● MK-20 ROCKEYE	490		6			6			6		18		−3 TO +7.33
TRAINING												700 KCAS M = 1.4	−2 TO +5
● SUU-20B/A	455		1			1			1		3		
FUEL TANK												660 KCAS M = 1.5	−2 TO +7.33
● 600 GALLON	4285		1			1			1		3		

GP76-0072-2

na down 15° and rotating left and right 45°. The radar reads the ground speed every 2.5 seconds and updates the Central Computer. In the air-to-ground ranging mode, the radar receives slant range measurements from various ground points. This mode is used primarily for bombing. The ground map mode uses low PRF pulse and reads the ground like conventional radar.

Once the master mode A/G button is pushed, the switches on the stick and throttle are ready to be used on the air-to-ground function. For example, the nose wheel steering button activates EO guided weapons once the A/G master mode is pressed.

The F-15 has six different modes for delivering ordnance. The important aspect of most of these modes is that they can be used with the Head-Up Display (HUD). With the exception of the ground map and EO ordnance, the pilot can press the attack without looking into the cockpit.

The F-15 can carry air-to-ground ordnance without affecting its ability to carry air-to-air missiles. In the past, certain fighter aircraft required the decision prior to flight as to what would be carried, e.g. bombs, missiles, extra tanks, etc. The F-15, however, requires no down loading of any missiles to put on ordnance nor does it require down loading of missiles to on-load ordnance.

Historically, most bomb racks have been limited to 5 g's. However, the F-15's MER-200 bomb racks can sustain a load factor of 7.33 g's. With these same bomb racks, the F-15 can operate at greater than Mach 1 at sea level, and up to Mach 1.4 at 20,000 feet. There are no primary air-to-ground weapons for the F-15 since it can carry any ordnance normally associated with an attack aircraft such as the A-7 or the A-10. Not only can the F-15 carry a plethora of air-to-ground ordnance, but in testing by the Air Force, they found the F-15 to be more accurate than the A-4E/F, A-7A/B, F-4D/E, A-7D/E, A-6A, or the F-111A/D.

If the pilot selects the 10 mile range while in LRS the radar goes automatically into the Short Range Search (SRS) mode. Short Range Search has a range of 10 miles, and provides detection and acquisition in all aspects since only medium PRF is transmitted in this mode. This is also the mode used for the AIM-9L and gun.

Finally, there remains the pulse search which is the old standby from World War II. All antenna scan patterns and ranges are available. The pulse waveform is low PRF.

All of the previous modes are manually selected on the radar mode selector. Since one of the F-15's strong suits is its ease of weapon

- Six different modes of delivery

MODE	PRIMARY USES	ADVANTAGES
Automatic	• Level, Dive, Dive Toss • Low and High Drag Weapons • Offset Bombing from IP	• Computed ballistics • Automatic Release to Minimize Pilot Error • Attack Steering • Maximum Flexibility of Attack Geometry with Multiple Ways to Designate
Continuously Displayed Impact Point	• Level, Dive • Low and High Drag Weapons • Multiple Targets on Single Pass	• Computed ballistics • Pilot Control of Release Initiation
Guided Weapon	• Long Stand-Off Ranges • Defended High-Contrast Targets	• Best Accuracy for Point Target
Direct	• Back Up - Provides Canned Delivery When Central Computer or HUD is Inoperative	
Manual	• Back Up - Provides Canned Delivery When Armament Control Set is Inoperative	
Ground Map	• Level, Dive, Dive Toss • Offset Bombing From IP	• Can be Used When The Target is in Adverse Weather Conditions

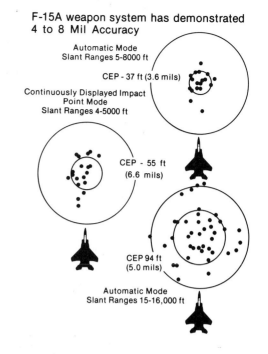

F-15A weapon system has demonstrated 4 to 8 Mil Accuracy

Automatic Mode
Slant Ranges 5-8000 ft

CEP - 37 ft (3.6 mils)

Continuously Displayed Impact Point Mode
Slant Ranges 4-5000 ft

CEP - 55 ft (6.6 mils)

CEP 94 ft (5.0 mils)

Automatic Mode
Slant Ranges 15-16,000 ft

system utilization by one pilot, the radar has an Automatic Mode which is selected by a flip of a switch on the same radar mode control panel. Once this switch is selected, the control of the radar requires only the selection of the weapon select switch on the throttle. The Central Computer automatically selects the radar parameters best suited for the weapon selected.

To complement the automatic mode selection, the F-15 has automatic acquisition switches on the control stick which are independent of either the manual or auto radar control switch. They are Supersearch and Boresight. Supersearch can acquire any target which appears within the HUD field of view. Supersearch has a 10 mile range with a scan pattern that covers the HUD for a 20° azimuth/ 6 bar combination. To command Supersearch the pilot pulls back on the Automatic Acquisi-

tion Switch. The radar automatically locks on and tracks the first target it sees.

Boresight is selected by pushing the automatic acquisition switch forward. In this mode any target within 10 miles along the boresight line of the F-15 will be acquired, and it can be done while the aircraft is any other air-to-air mode. This allows the pilot to fly in a general search mode, be surprised by a threat, and handle the matter by pointing the nose of the aircraft at the threat, push forward on the auto acquisition switch and fire either a *Sparrow, Sidewinder,* or the gun. In the F-4 the pilot would have had to look inside the cockpit and start fiddling with time consuming switches all to his detriment. In Boresight, if the radar was transmitting in low PRF pulse before boresight was selected, it will continue to do so while in boresight, otherwise the boresight mode will transmit in medium PRF.

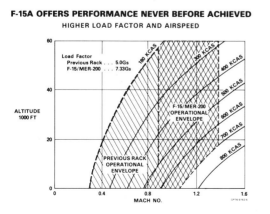

F-15A OFFERS PERFORMANCE NEVER BEFORE ACHIEVED
HIGHER LOAD FACTOR AND AIRSPEED

Load Factor
Previous Rack . . . 5.0Gs
F-15/MER-200 . . . 7.33Gs

F-15/MER-200 OPERATIONAL ENVELOPE

PREVIOUS RACK OPERATIONAL ENVELOPE

ALTITUDE 1000 FT

MACH NO.

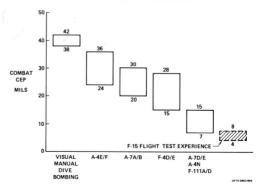

WEAPON DELIVERY ACCURACY

COMBAT CEP MILS

42 / 38 — VISUAL MANUAL DIVE BOMBING
36 / 24 — A-4E/F
30 / 20 — A-7A/B
28 / 15 — F-4D/E
15 / 7 — A-7D/E, A-4N, F-111A/D
8 / 4 — F-15 FLIGHT TEST EXPERIENCE

A TF-15, now F-15B, loaded with three nuclear Mk 57 bombs with 15 to 20 kiloton yield. The Mk 57 is also known as the B-57, and the inert practice version is known as the BDU-11E. (McDonald Douglas)

Nuclear Delivery. *3 Mk 57 nuclear tactical weapons and 4 AIM-7F* Sparrow *missiles.*

Strike. *26 Mk 82 low drag bombs, 4 AIM-9L* Sidewinder *missiles, and FAST Pack with fuel.*

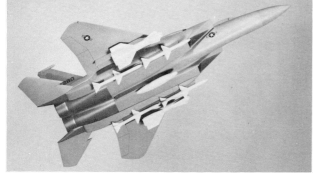

Advanced strike. *2 GBU-15 Cruciform and Guidance Pod, 4 AIM-7F* Sparrow *missiles, and FAST Packs with fuel.*

Strike. *5 Mk 84 lazer guided bombs, ECM pods, 4 AIM-9L* Sidewinder *missiles and FAST Pack with fuel.*

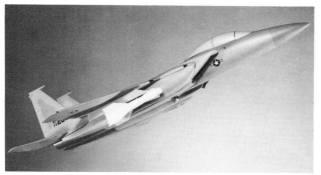

Advanced strike. *2 GBU-15, Internal Forward Looking Infrared/EO, and FAST Pack with fuel.*

A close-up of the ordnance carrying capability of the F-15 shows how air-to-ground weapons can be up-loaded and down-loaded without affecting the aircraft's air-to-air capability.

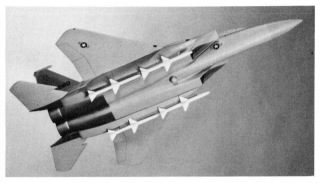

Advanced strike minus air-to-ground *(4 AIM-7F Sparrow missiles and FAST Packs with fuel).*

Strike Suppression. *3 HARMS, Self-defense (4 AIM-7F Sparrows, 4 AIM-9L Sidewinder and 20mm gun), ECM Pods, and FAST Pack with fuel.*

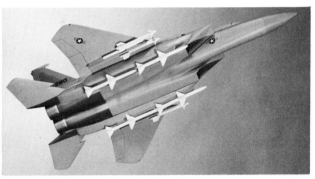

Interceptor or Basic Air Superiority. *4 AIM-7F Sparrow missiles, 4 AIM-9L Sidewinder missiles, and FAST Packs with fuel.*

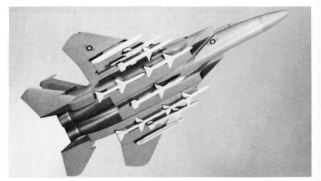

Advanced Strike. *3 SRAMs, 2 ALCMs, 4 AIM-9L Sidewinder missiles and FAST Pack.*

Advanced Intercepter. *6 AIM-54 Phoenix missiles, 2 AIM-9L Sidewinder missiles, and FAST Packs.*

Sea Surveillance. *4 Harpoon missiles and FAST Packs.*

(McDonnell Douglas)

Specifications

Length:	2.9m (113 in.)
Diameter:	0.12m (5 in.)
Wing Span:	0.63m (25 in.)
Canard Span:	0.4m (22.3 in.)
Weight:	86 kg (190 lb)
Guidance:	Passive Infrared
Warhead:	10.15 kg (25 lb)
Fuzing:	Proximity and Contact
Launcher:	Rail

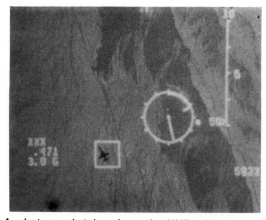

A photograph taken from the HUD with the gun selected shows the radar locked on an F-5E in the target designator box. The F-15 is flying at Mach .471 and pulling 3.9 g's. The 50 next to the vertical range indicator shows that the rate of closure is 50 knots. (McDonnell Douglas)

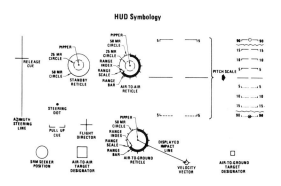

The nomenclature for the Head-Up Display (HUD) is shown above. (McDonnell Douglas)

The opening to the M61 20mm Vulcan cannon on the right wing root. (McDonnell Douglas)

Weapons

The three primary air-to-air weapons for the F-15 are the AIM-7F *Sparrow* medium range radar guided missile, the AIM-9E and L *Sidewinder* short range heat seeking missile, and the M-61 20mm cannon, with 940 rounds of ammunition.

AIM-7F Sparrow

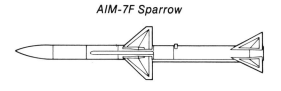

Length:	3.65m	Guidance:	Radar-Semiactive Continuous Wave (CW)	
Diameter:	0.2m	Navigation:	Proportional Homing	
Wingspan:	1.0m	Warhead:	30 kg hi-explosive	
Tailspan:	0.8m	Fuzing:	Proximity and Contact	
Weight:	200 kg	Launcher:	Rail, Ejection, or Cell	

An ALQ-119 ECM pod is carried on the outboard wing pylon. Only ECM equipment is carried on this outer pulon. (McDonnell Douglas)

An underside view of an F-15A with two wing tanks. (McDonnell Douglas)

Mission

The mission of the F-15 falls into perspective once the mission of the U.S. Air Force, and the Air Force major commands are known. Aerospace operations have four major categories: strategic, tactical, special and combat support. These categories are further broken down into:

1. Strategic attack
2. Counter-air
3. Air interdiction
4. Close air support
5. Aerospace defense of the United States
6. Aerospace surveillance and reconnaissance
7. Airlift, and
8. Special operations.

Of all these the F-15 was produced initially with the role of counter air in mind. However, the *Eagle* is subsequently proving to having strong capabilities in air interdiction, aerospace defense of the U.S. and aerospace surveillance and reconnaissance.

Counter air is usually thought of as operations designed to acquire and maintain air superiority by offensive and defensive operations. Offensively, in counter air operations, aircraft seek out and destroy targets that would be used to help the enemy in its pursuit of the battle. Defensively, counter air operations are a response to the enemy's initiation to attempt to enter friendly air space.

Air interdiction is the mission normally thought of belonging to an attack plane or light bomber. This mission is offensive in nature with the purpose of finding the enemy and destroying its capability locally by eliminating equipment and communication. This mission is different from strategic attack, in that the latter is designed to destroy the will of an entire country, while air interdiction is localized and not on as large a scale.

Aerospace defense of the United States is straight forward. The mission is to protect the U.S. from incoming attack from missiles and bombers. The defense against incoming bomber's mission has typically belonged to the Aerospace Defense Command, one of the major commands under the Department of the Air Force. The mission currently is typically carried out by ADC's F-106s.

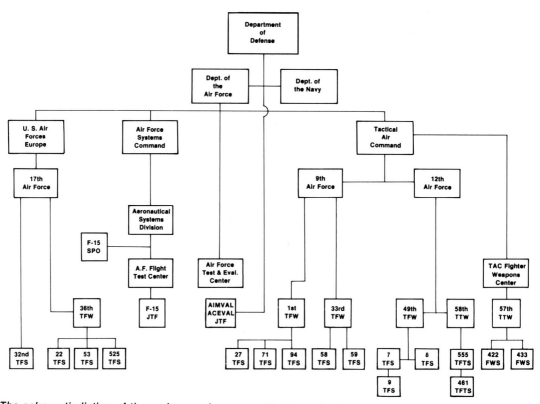

The schematic listing of the various major groups that have had a major role in the development and deployment of the F-15, is listed above. While not a complete list, it covers the major groups, and will allow a point of departure for anyone wishing to explore the organizational tables involved with the F-15 in detail.

The fourth major area that the F-15 fits comfortably into is aerospace surveillance and reconnaissance. The F-15 has the capabilities and growth potential to fulfill the requirements of tactical reconnaissance with real-time maps from very high resolution radar and other sensors, strike coverage, weather information, and aerial mapping.

To provide these and the other missions, the U. S. Air Force is divided into major commands. These major commands are either functional or geographical. A functional command—for example the Strategic Air Command—has the same duty wherever it is located. A geographical command's—an example is U. S. Air Forces Europe (USAFE)—responsibility is contained within geographical boundaries. During the development of the F-15 the Air Force Systems Command (AFCS)—a functional command—was responsible for the development and testing of the then FX and ultimately F-15. Delivery of the first F-15 was to the Tactical Air Command (TAC). The first overseas units will come under the control of the U.S. Air Forces Europe (USAFE).

The primary user of the F-15 now and for the foreseeable future is the Tactical Air Command (TAC) and the corresponding commands, USAFE and PACAF. TAC is the U.S.'s mobile strike force with the responsibility of responding world-wide. TAC became a separate command on March 21, 1946. Temporarily known as Strike Command, TAC is located at Langley AFB, Virginia where it directs the activities of the 9th Air Force, located at Shaw AFB, South Carolina and the 12th Air Force at Bergstrom AFB, Texas. TAC's six major areas of operation are counterair, air interdiction, tactical air reconnaissance, close air support, tactical airlift and tactical electronic warfare. The first three are directly associated with the F-15.

The first squadron to receive the F-15 was the 555th Tactical Fighter Training Squadron of the 58th Tactical Fighter Training Wing, now known as the 58th Tactical Training Wing. TAC 1, as the first F-15 (in reality a TF-15) to enter the Tactical Air Command was called, arrived on November 14, 1974 with 73-108 painted on its tail. A sister squadron, the 461st TFTS, was formed shortly thereafter. These two squadrons, the 555th TFTS and the 461st TFTS have the responsibility of training new pilots out of the training command, as well as veteran pilots transitioning to the F-15.

The first F-15 for the 1st TFW lands at Langley AFB, Virginia, January 9, 1976 with Lt. Col. Richard L. Craft, commanding officer of the 27th TFS at the controls. *(USAF)*

The first operational Tatical Air Command wing is the 1st Tactical Fighter Wing (TFW) at Langley AFB, Virginia. Langley received their first F-15 on January 9, 1976 when Lt. Col. Richard L. Craft, Commander of the 27th TFS landed F-15 serial number 74-083. The 1st TFW traces its history back to the 1st Pursuit Group of World War I. The 1st TFW has three squadrons. The 27th Tactical Fighter Squadron (TFS) was the squadron that Frank Luke, the WWI ace, belonged to. The 94th TFS produced 12 aces during World War I including Eddie Rickenbacker. The 71st TFS originally designated 71st Pursuit Squadron on 14 December 1940, is the third Tactical Fighter Squadron of the 1st TFW.

The second operational Tactical Fighter Wing is the 36th TFW located at Bittburg, Germany. Under the 17th Air Force, the 36th TFW is the first F-15 wing to operate under the geographical command of the U.S. Air Forces Europe. The 36th TFW received their first two F-15s, serial numbers 75-0049 and 75-0050 on January 5, 1977 sent over for training and familiarization, but first group of 23 aircraft were flown en masse on April 27, 1977. The 36th TFW is made up of the 525th TFS, 22nd TFS and the 53rd TFS. Before augmenting to the F-15, the 36th was flying F-4Es.

The next scheduled wing to receive the F-15 is the 49th TFW at Holloman AFB in New Mexico. The three squadrons to fly the *Eagle* are 7th TFS, 8th TFS, and 9th TFS.

In addition to the operational tasks of the 1st, 36th, 49th TFW, 33rd and 32nd TFS, and the training responsibility of the 58th TTW, the 57th Tactical Training Wing has two specialized squadrons under it. The 57th TTW comes under the U.S. Air Force Tactical Fighter Weapons Center (TFWC) which reports directly to TAC headquarters. Under the 57th TTW falls the 422nd Fighter Weapons Squadron which is charged with the Follow on Operation Test and Evaluation (FOT&E) previously known as Category III for all the Air Force tactical fighter aircraft. Whenever a new program develops to test a modification, or to maintain an ongoing test program, it is done by the 422nd FWS. To develop experts in the F-15 the 433rd Fighter Weapons Squadron will put one 433rd FWS graduate in each squadron of F-15s. The 433rd FWS was formed on October 1, 1976 by special order GA-20 Tactical Air Command, dated May 21, 1976. The squadron assumed the number and history of the 433rd Tactical Fighter Squadron which was deactivated at Ubon, Thailand on July 23, 1974. The squadron received their first aircraft on November 10,

1976 when the commander, Lt. Col. Dave Jacobsen, landed at Nellis AFB with *Eagle* serial number 75-0042. Scheduled for six aircraft, the other five and their dates of arrival were:

Date	Serial Number
30 November 1976	75-0043
13 December 1976	75-0084 (TF)
21 December 1976	75-0054
22 December 1976	75-0085 (TF)
1 January 1977	75-0055

developed software for the ACMI which shows the flight trajectory and range of each missile, and the probability of kill (P_k). To add to the realism they have also programmed in failures in the missiles so that pilots may not get a shot due to a programmed failure in the missile. The ACEVAL portion of the program will test combinations of aircraft and evaluate tactical maneuvers. Up until ACMR—a first generation of the ACMI—who shot who was always a question of drink or rank. The pilot with the most to drink or the most rank usually won. The Air

An AIMVAL/ACEVAL F-15 with "concept" missiles under the right wing.   (McDonnell Douglas)

The purpose of the 433rd FWS is to make each of its graduates experts in the F-15. The four month classes are small with four to six students per class, three classes per year. The emphasis is on a complete understanding of the physical and aerodynamic characteristics as well as the tactical deployment of the F-15. The 433rd's first class began January 1978.

The F-15 is also involved in a joint Navy and Air Force Department of Defense program known as AIMVAL/ACEVAL. AIMVAL is an acronym for air intercept missile (AIM) evaluation; ACEVAL is an acronym for air combat evaluation. The AIMVAL/ACEVAL program is authorized for 10 months, beginning in January 1977 and running through late September and early October of that same year. During the AIMVAL portion, both F-14s and F-15s will be evaluating current and future missiles, results of which will be analyzed on the Cubic Corporation Air Combat Maneuvering Instrumentation (ACMI). Programmers have

Combat Maneuvering Range took away the guesswork on smaller engagements. However, the ACMR equipment was limited to the numbers of planes. The ACMI equipment located at Nellis AFB can take larger number of engagements and render more information.

The AIMVAL/ACEVAL program is, if not distorted by statisticians with a political bent, the culmination of over 60 years of fighter aviation in that all that has been learned from previous wars will now be quantified under the eyes of hundreds of analysts.

The good guys in this program are the F-14s and F-15s and are called the Blue Force and the bad guys flying F-5Es on loan from Nellis Agressor Squadrons are called the Red Force. The F-5E was picked to represent the threat because its flight characteristics are like a MiG-21, its size is approximately the same, and it is a dissimilar aircraft.

Some changes were made to the AIMVAL/ACEVAL F-15s which are supposed to be representative of changes that will be

Air Force Test and Evaluation (AFTEC) F-15s returning to Luke AFB from Edwards AFB after an elevation of AIM-7Fs. Air Superiority Blue and compass Ghost Grey paint schemes are mixed, 26 June 1976.

(Jim Posgate)

made in the operation squadron aircraft. In fact, one of the ground rules is that the Blue Force aircraft must fly with equipment that will be quickly implemented into the operation squadrons. There were several hardware changes. The F-15s have added Visual Identification Target Acquisition System (VITAS) which is a helmet mounted eyepiece that when placed on the target activates the weapon system. The addition of an LAU-7 to hold the SS-2 concept missile was a necessary change that will not necessarily be part of the operational aircraft. The AIMVAL/ACEVAL F-15s have two lights on the canopy: one to tell the pilot that the radar is locked on and the other to indicate that he is in the envelope for both the AIM-7F and AIM-9L. These two lights were added so that the pilot would have this information without looking back into the cockpit.

There were some software changes to the F-15 radar computer too. To accommodate the new missiles, the F-15 Blue Force removed the air-to-ground program from the radar computer and replaced it with a program that lets the computer talk with the VITAS and the SS-1 and SS-2 concept missiles. The ability to search while track (SWT) was added which is similar to the track while scan (TWS) in the F-14, the difference being the F-15 has a single shot capability with the *Sparrow* while the F-14 has the multi-shot with the *Phoenix* missile. The last major software change is Expand Mode (EM) which expands in azimuth and range 5

miles around the target to show whether the one target represented is really one, or if there are others. Before Expand Mode, two targets 25 miles away had to be 1½ miles apart to be seen as two targets. EM can see 2 targets 500 feet apart at 20 miles.

In March 1975, four months after the introduction of the F-15 to TAC at Luke AFB, the Air Force Test and Evaluation Center (AFTEC) took on the responsibility of Category III testing. Now known as Follow-on Operational Test and Evaluation (FOT&E), AFTEC's mission was for an independent analysis of the F-15, with the results going directly to the Chief of Staff of the Air Force. The aircraft was lent to the FOT&E group from the 57th TTW at Nellis. The operations took place at Luke AFB with Luke providing the maintenance. The test team was composed of a director, Lt. Col. Art Bergman, USAF, with 5 pilots from TAC, one from Aerospace Defense Command, and one from Air Force Systems Command. The operational test force had six F-15As and one TF-15A which was in fact the first TF-15 assigned to TAC, TF-3 or TAC 1. In pursuing its design mission of independent analysis, the Operation Test Force (OTF) flew approximately 1,100 sorties. They flew against high and fast targets at Edwards AFB, used the radar against multiple threats at Nellis AFB, flew ACM against multiple aircraft including the Navy Fighter Weapons School at Yuma MCAS, and tested the gun at Eglin AFB in Florida.

RF-15 CONFIGURATION

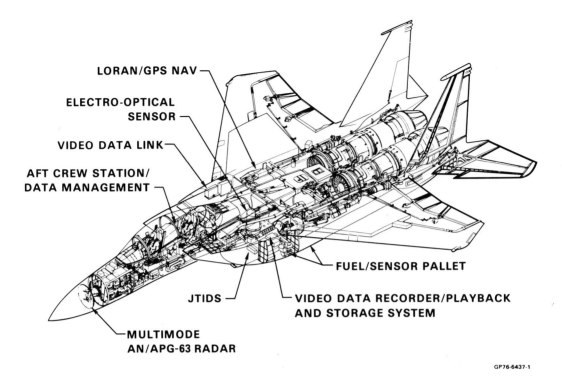

LORAN/GPS NAV

ELECTRO-OPTICAL SENSOR

VIDEO DATA LINK

AFT CREW STATION/ DATA MANAGEMENT

FUEL/SENSOR PALLET

JTIDS

VIDEO DATA RECORDER/PLAYBACK AND STORAGE SYSTEM

MULTIMODE AN/APG-63 RADAR

GP76-6437-1

Future Versions

The F-15 lends itself to additonal versions because of the additional internal volume available, excess thrust, and weapon system design. The F-15 has an additional 77 cubic feet of internal drag-free space which is suitable for additional fuel or other mission requirements. The generators can produce 50 KVA additional electricity over what is currently needed. The Central Computer has additional growth capability. Because of the software designed weapon system, the addition of new ordnance requires no changes in aircraft hardware.

The most significant system of the F-15 which lends itself to new versions is the FAST PACKs. The FAST PACK, which stands for *Fuel And Sensor Tactical Package*, adds an additional 227 cubic feet of space for fuel, augmented thrust, cargo, reconnaissance missions, or electronic counter measures equipment. The two FAST PACKs can carry 1538 gallons of fuel which is 28 percent more fuel than two external fuel tanks, and only 17 percent less fuel than the three external tanks. One of the benefits of the FAST PACK conformal

tanks is that they don't interrupt an underwing storage for air-to-air or air-to-ground missions. Ironically, the F-15 with these conformal FAST PACKs has the same subsonic cruise drag as the total F-15 drag is without them.

The most probable new version of the F-15 would be as an interceptor for the Aerospace Defense Command (ADCOM). The F-15 would be a logical choice for the Air Force because of the common engine, and because any changes can probably be done in the Central Computer.

With the introduction of the F-15 into the Air Force inventory and the gradual phasing out of the F-4 *Phantom*, the need for a reconnaissance version of the F-15 seems imminent. McDonnell Douglas has developed an RF-15 on paper with significant increases in usable information for the tactical field commander.

New advances in airborne radar can permit the F-15, and ultimately the people on the ground who have to analyze the data, much more detail from radar mapping. A new technique called Synthetic Aperature Radar (SAR), can look through clouds and other in-

F-15 with Internal FLIR/EO, FAST PACKS with Fw'd Oblique Camera, Split Vertical Camera plus SLAR.
(McDonnell Douglas)

CREW STATION

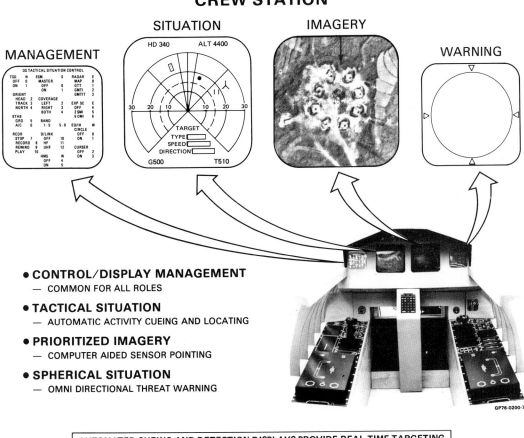

- **CONTROL/DISPLAY MANAGEMENT**
  - COMMON FOR ALL ROLES

- **TACTICAL SITUATION**
  - AUTOMATIC ACTIVITY CUEING AND LOCATING

- **PRIORITIZED IMAGERY**
  - COMPUTER AIDED SENSOR POINTING

- **SPHERICAL SITUATION**
  - OMNI DIRECTIONAL THREAT WARNING

AUTOMATED CUEING AND DETECTION DISPLAYS PROVIDE REAL-TIME TARGETING

An F-15B with FAST Pack (F-15D in production) and 3 external tanks would allow it to make long flights like those illustrated on page 91.

(McDonnell Douglas)

FUEL PALLET/DROP TANK DRAG COMPARISON

- NO INCREASE IN SUBSONIC DRAG (OVER BASIC AIRCRAFT)
- MUCH LESS DRAG WITH PALLETS THAN WITH THE EXTERNAL FUEL TANKS

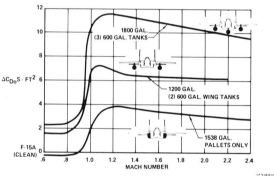

1800 GAL.
(3) 600 GAL. TANKS

1200 GAL.
(2) 600 GAL. WING TANKS

1538 GAL.
PALLETS ONLY

$\Delta c_{D_o}S - FT^2$

F-15A (CLEAN)

MACH NUMBER

GP74-4439-55

DESIGN FLEXIBILITY/PALLET INSTALLATION

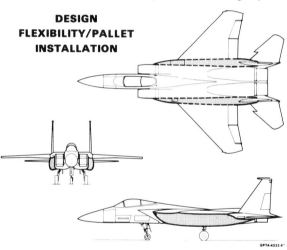

GP74-4222-6

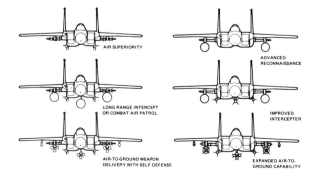

AIR SUPERIORITY

ADVANCED RECONNAISSANCE

LONG RANGE INTERCEPT OR COMBAT AIR PATROL

IMPROVED INTERCEPTER

AIR-TO-GROUND WEAPON DELIVERY WITH SELF DEFENSE

EXPANDED AIR-TO-GROUND CAPABILITY

FAST PACK EXPANDS MISSION CAPABILITIES . . .
. . . WITH MINIMUM CHANGE

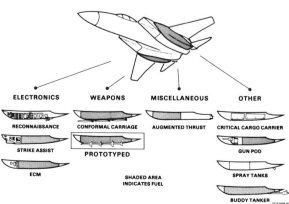

ELECTRONICS

RECONNAISSANCE

STRIKE ASSIST

ECM

WEAPONS

CONFORMAL CARRIAGE

PROTOTYPED

MISCELLANEOUS

AUGMENTED THRUST

SHADED AREA INDICATES FUEL

OTHER

CRITICAL CARGO CARRIER

GUN POD

SPRAY TANKS

BUDDY TANKER

GP74-4439-34

One of the contract requirements of the F-15 was to be able to
fly trans-Atlantic non-stop unrefueled. The Israelis that made
the raid on Entebbe could have flown from Israel to Entebbe
with conformal tanks (FAST Packs) and three external tanks
non-stop and without refueling. On arrival, the F-15 would
have enough fuel to loiter overhead for an hour—the length of
the "Raid"—and still have enough fuel to divert to a friendly
country.
(McDonnell Douglas)

FERRY FLIGHT TO EUROPE
FAST PACK + (3) 600 GAL. EXTERNAL TANKS

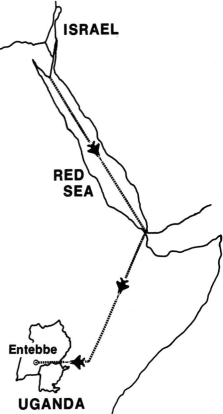

2650 NM IN 5 HOURS, 15 MINUTES

41,000 FT
4 HR. 59 MIN.
3,800 LB FUEL
REMAINING

33,000 FT

BENTWATERS,
ENGLAND
LANDING
1919 GMT

LORING
AFB
TAKEOFF
0604 EDT

TAKE OFF GROSS WEIGHT	65,979 LB
FUEL – INTERNAL	11,177 LB
– EXTERNAL	11,529 LB
– FAST PACK	9,613 LB
TOTAL	32,319 LB

ISRAEL

RED
SEA

Entebbe

UGANDA

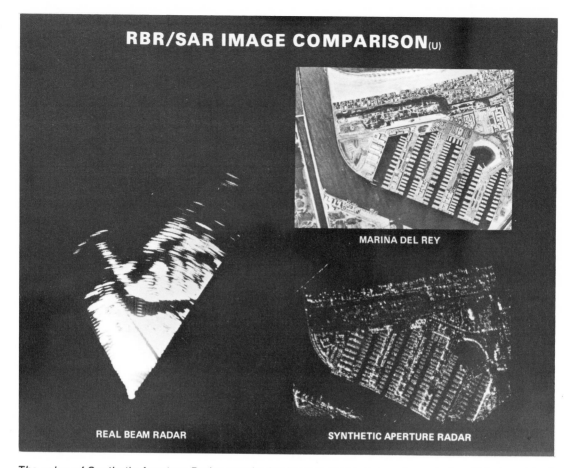

RBR/SAR IMAGE COMPARISON(U)

MARINA DEL REY

REAL BEAM RADAR

SYNTHETIC APERTURE RADAR

The value of Synthetic Aperture Radar speaks for itself in these comparison photos. This type of advanced avionic capability results from software computer changes. **(McDonnell Douglas)**

hibiting visual phenomenon to get resolutions down to 20 feet. Since every seventh F-15 is planned as a TF-15, the two-seat requirement for a reconnaissance version of the F-15 is pre-ordained. The APG-63 radar has the necessary elements to incorporate these high resolution techniques. With a slight modification, the APG-63 can include Ground Moving Target Indication (GMTI) and Terrain Following (TF) modes, without increasing the radar space or volume.

SYSTEM OPERATOR STATION
AFT COCKPIT

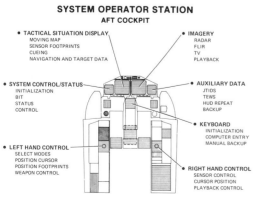

- TACTICAL SITUATION DISPLAY
  MOVING MAP
  SENSOR FOOTPRINTS
  CUEING
  NAVIGATION AND TARGET DATA

- SYSTEM CONTROL/STATUS
  INITIALIZATION
  BIT
  STATUS
  CONTROL

- LEFT HAND CONTROL
  SELECT MODES
  POSITION CURSOR
  POSITION FOOTPRINTS
  WEAPON CONTROL

- IMAGERY
  RADAR
  FLIR
  TV
  PLAYBACK

- AUXILIARY DATA
  JTIDS
  TEWS
  HUD REPEAT
  BACKUP

- KEYBOARD
  INITIALIZATION
  COMPUTER ENTRY
  MANUAL BACKUP

- RIGHT HAND CONTROL
  SENSOR CONTROL
  CURSOR POSITION
  PLAYBACK CONTROL

GP77-0017-4

After all the descriptions of the capability of the F-15 have been given, it's reasonable to wonder how the F-15 has actually done carrying out its assigned mission. Since the F-15 has the design characteristics of both an interceptor and clear air mass dogfighter, there is data to report on these different missions.

In a beyond visual range evaluation, four F-15s participated in a large-scale tactical exercise at Edwards AFB, California between April 29, 1974 and May 14th of the same year. The F-15 flew against MiG-23 *Flogger* simulators (F-4E) and against MiG-21 *Fishbed* simulators (F-5E). The F-15 won 45 out of 46 engagements. The F-15 launched 296 missiles compared to 18 for the overall adversary.

In September 1974, four Israeli pilots and one radar operator flew TF-1 at Edwards AFB, California for three days of evaluation. None of the Israeli pilots had ever flown the F-15 before. The Israeli's were able to perform the following ACM maneuvers against a slatted F-4E.

F-15 AIR COMBAT MANEUVERS
CONVERSION BY OUT TURNING AND ACCELERATING

F-4E   F-15

F-4E STARTS 1000 FT BEHIND F-15
CO-SPEED AT 170 KCAS AND
12,000 FT ALTITUDE

F-4E OVERSHOT
F-15 ACHIEVED
TRACKING POSITION

F-15 AIR COMBAT MANEUVERS
MANEUVERED TO TRACKING PRIOR
TO F-4 COMPLETING 360° TURN
ANTIPARALLEL STARTING CONDITION

300 KCAS AT 10,000 FT   F-4E

F-15 ACHIEVED
GUN FIRING
POSITION PRIOR TO
F-4E COMPLETING
360° OF TURN

300 KCAS
AT 10,000 FT

F-15

GP75 5196 5

F-15 AIR COMBAT MANEUVERS
MANEUVERED INSIDE F-4 FROM PARALLEL START CONDITIONS

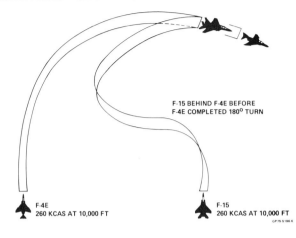

F-15 BEHIND F-4E BEFORE
F-4E COMPLETED 180° TURN

F-4E
260 KCAS AT 10,000 FT

F-15
260 KCAS AT 10,000 FT

GP75 5196 6

Upper and lower left. *The two upper and lower left illustrations show the maneuverability that is possible with the F-15* Eagle *in Air Combat Maneuvering (ACM) against the F-4* Phantom. *These particular illustrations were generated as a result of the Israeli Air Force evaluation team's experience in one-on-one "dogfights" against an F-4E. It was through Israeli prodding that the F-15 was demonstrated to produce a loop at 150 knots.*

The F-15 has been used in five AWACS demonstrations: Edwards AFB, California in October 1974; Europe in April 1975, Washington State in May 1975, Luke AFB in November 1976 and Washington State in December 1976. In the California and Washington State exercise, threat-simulating aircraft used Electronic Counter Measures as well as the other inherent capabilities. The F-15 prevailed 38 of 39 intercepts and was able to fly 13 flights without any squawk.

It is this kind of capability that allowed the F-15 during its Category III testing at Luke AFB by the Air Force Test and Evaluation Center to travel to various air bases and prevail during air combat maneuvering. Typical of the F-15's successes is the following printout from the ACMR (Air Combat Maneuvering Range) near Marine Corps Air Station Yuma.

TYPICAL AWACS DEFENSE MISSION

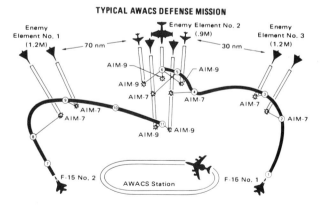

Enemy Element No. 1 (1.2M)

Enemy Element No. 2 (.9M)

Enemy Element No. 3 (1.2M)

70 nm   30 nm

AIM-9

AIM-9

AIM-9

AIM-7

AIM-7

AIM-7

AIM-7

AIM-7

AIM-7

AIM-9

AIM-9

F-15 No. 2

AWACS Station

F-15 No. 1

A typical F-15/AWACS Mission shows the coordination between the E-3A AWACS aircraft and two F-15s. Although the F-15s are outnumbered 1 v. 9, F-15 No. 2 still has 2 AIM-7Fs, and 2 AIM-9Ls; F-15 No. 1 has 1 AIM-9L left. Neither F-15 has fired its M61 20mm gun which has 960 rounds.

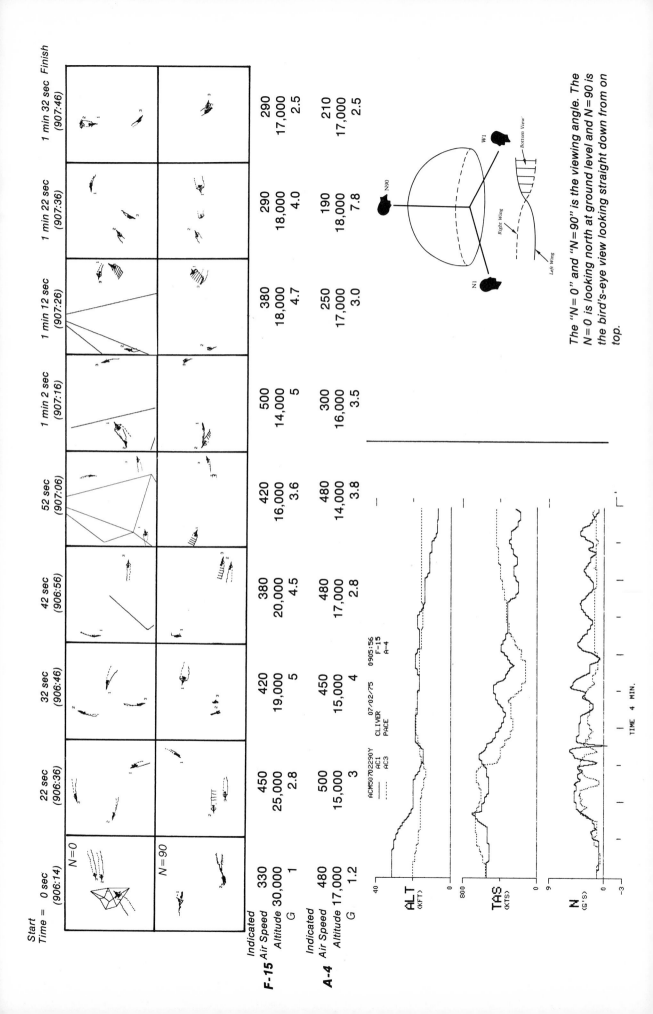

The "N = 0" and "N = 90" is the viewing angle. The N = 0 is looking north at ground level and N = 90 is the bird's-eye view looking straight down from on top.

These two pages represent a print-out from the ACMR of a dogfight between Major Jeff Cliver USAF in an F-15 *Eagle* and two A-4 *Mongooses* flown by LCDR Jim Ruliffson USN and LT Dave Pace USN from the Navy Fighter Weapons School. The F-15 defeated both A-4s, but for lack of space, the concentration is on the A-4 flown by LT Pace. The charts below the aircraft show the information generated by Major Cliver's and LT Pace's aircraft. Major Cliver is in the aircraft marked "1" and LT Pace is in the aircraft marked "3."

The X-Y plots below the print-out of the dogfight give a complete history of the status of both aircraft during the fight. Information such as the altitude of both aircraft during the history of the flight, the relative velocity, the true airspeed and more is shown in these charts. The various symbols mean:

ALT = Altitude in thousands of feet
TAS = True airspeed in knots
N = Number of g's the aircraft is pulling
V$_C$ = Velocity of closure
E$_s$ = Specific energy in feet
P$_s$ = Specific excess power in feet/second
T rate = Turn rate in degrees/second
T rad = Turn radius in thousands of feet
R = Relative distance in thousands of feet
AOT = Angle off the tail in degrees

Occasionally the lines on the graph will jump up. This is probably a malfunction in the ACMR pod that transmits the information back to the computer.

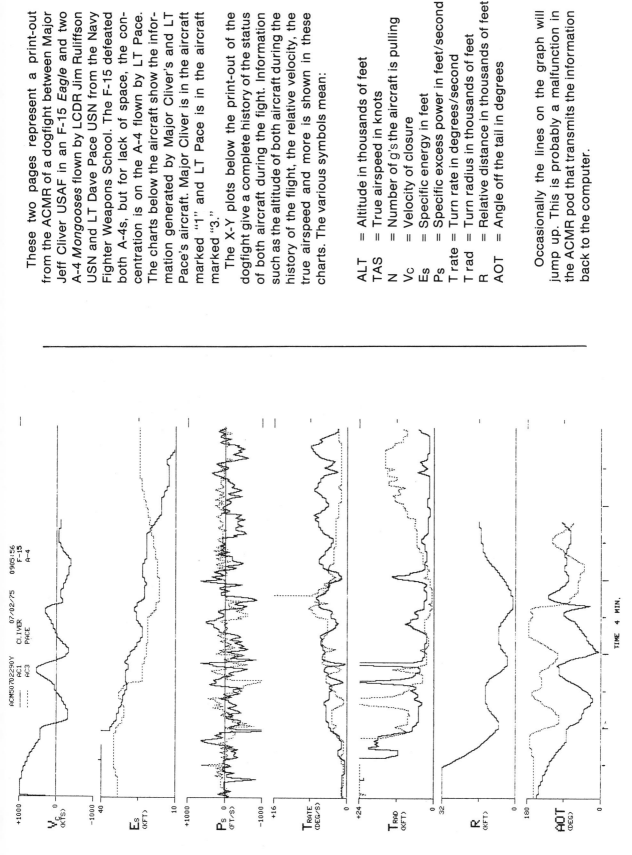

An artist's concept of how a Saudi Arabian F-15 Eagle *would look. As of early 1978 the Saudis are scheduled to receive 60 F-15s.* *(McDonnell Douglas)*

The ACMR has a series of antennas placed over a large area of land. These antennas receive signals from a pod which is carried on the aircraft where the AIM-7F *Sparrow* would ordinarily attach. By the use of large computers and complicated formulas, the ACMR can determine the position of each aircraft carrying an ACMR pod. These signals are then presented on a screen which shows the presentation of the dogfight from any angle. By turning the dials in from off the screen, the controller can rotate the fight so that he can look at the fight from any position around at 360° circle on the ground, or from any position from the ground up to a position of looking straight down on the fight.

What follows is a print-out of the fight between Major Jeff Cliver, USAF—a member of the FOT&E group from Luke AFB—flying the F-15, and two A-4 *Mongoose* (a stripped-down A-4E) flown by LCDR Jim Ruliffson, USN, then Commanding Officer of the Navy Fighter Weapons School, and LT Dave Pace, USN. Outnumbered two to one, the F-15 was able to handle both of these A-4s in the encounter that follows.

From the beginning, many critics of the F-15 asked if it had the capabilities of the MiG-25. The MiG-25 has the ability to fly at 80,000 feet and at speeds approaching Mach 3. The F-15 has the ability to cruise at altitudes in the low sixty thousand feet ranges, and at speeds of Mach 2.3. The F-15 can dash out to Mach 2.5, but only for a limited time. The actual Mach number that the MiG-25 can cruise at has been questioned as a result of the redline on the Mach meter of the MiG-25 flown to Japan in September 1976.

The MiG-25 was never intended to do more than act as a high altitude interceptor against the then expected threat of the B-70. The real point defense threat is the Su-15 *Flagon*, and, at medium and low altitudes, the air superiority of the MiG-23 *Flogger*.

Nevertheless, the F-15 is capable of intercepting a MiG-25 within a minute once notified of its existence. In June 1976, the Air Force downed two drones simulating MiG-25s. The first missile was fired at a Bomarc drone flying at Mach 2.7 at 71,000 feet. The missile, which was unarmed, passed within lethal distance of the target. The second missile, which was armed, hit a Bomarc which, traveling at Mach 2.7 and 68,000 feet, made a direct hit. These, and other simulated Foxbat intercepts, have demonstrated that the improved *Sparrow*, the AIM-7F, combined with the altitude capabilities of the F-15 and its long range radar, are capable of downing a MiG-25 with ease.

The F-15, which first flew in July 1972, was introduced into the Air Force inventory in November 1974. The ability to meet the needed improvements of tomorrow has been designed in by the use of software computer systems. It seems clear from the designed-in flexibility and unused space that the F-15 will be in the U. S. Air Force inventory for a long time.

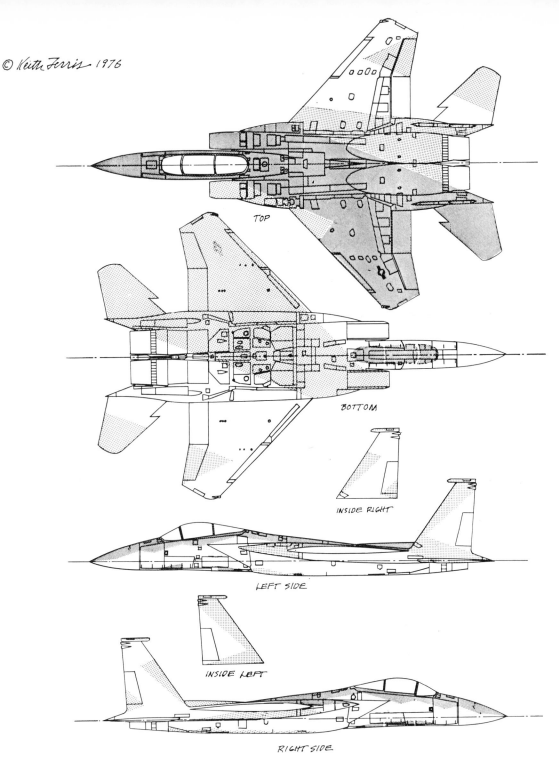

© Keith Ferris 1976

TOP

BOTTOM

INSIDE RIGHT

LEFT SIDE

INSIDE LEFT

RIGHT SIDE

The Keith Ferris paint scheme seen on several F-15s. Ferris, an aviation artist, invented the paint scheme after having difficulty painting WWII aircraft which were painted to make detection in the air difficult. All camouflage schemes have been designed to make detection on the ground—or slightly off the ground—difficult. The Ferris scheme is the first attempt to make attitude detection difficult in the Air Combat Maneuvering arena.

Four F-15s were painted in the Ferris Attitude Deception scheme. These planes were stationed at Luke AFB, Arizona.

	Federal Standard Number			
AF Serial Number	Light	Medium	Dark	Canopy
74-0110	36622	36440	36231	36231
74-0089	36440	36231	36320	36118
74-0139	36440	36231	36118	36118
73-0111	36440*	36231	36118	36118

*Anywhere 36440 appears on top - approximates 36320 (mix 36440 with 36231)

97

LEVEL FLIGHT ENVELOPE

AIRPLANE CONFIGURATION
- (1) CLEAN (GROSS WEIGHT 33,000 LB)
- (2) (4) AIM–7F MISSILES (GROSS WEIGHT 35,040 LB)

REMARKS
ENGINE(S): (2) F100–PW–100
U. S. STANDARD DAY, 1966

DATE: 1 JULY 1974
DATA BASIS: **ESTIMATED**

FUEL GRADE: JP–4
FUEL DENSITY: 6.5 LB/GAL

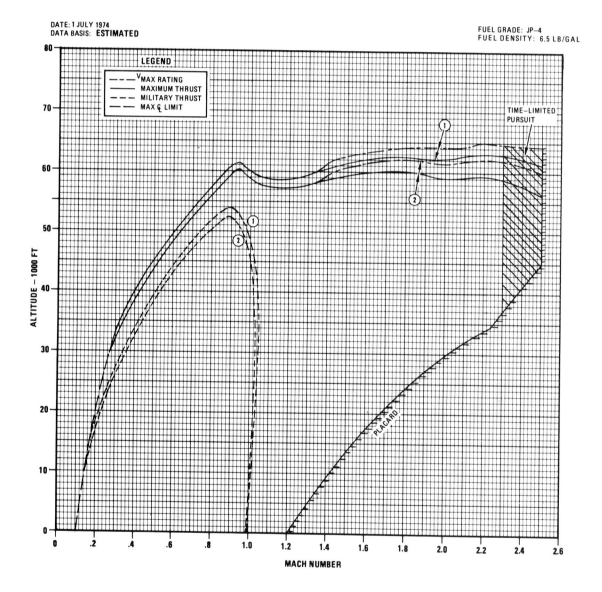

LEGEND
- – – – ^{V}MAX RATING
- ——— MAXIMUM THRUST
- – – – MILITARY THRUST
- – – – MAX C_L LIMIT

TIME–LIMITED PURSUIT

PLACARD

ALTITUDE – 1000 FT

MACH NUMBER

TIME TO CLIMB
MAXIMUM THRUST

REMARKS
ENGINE(S): (2) F100—PW—100
U.S. STANDARD DAY, 1966

AIRPLANE CONFIGURATION
INDIVIDUAL DRAG INDEXES

NOTES

● CLIMB SPEED SCHEDULE IS 350 KCAS UNTIL INTERCEPTION OF
0.95 MACH, THEN MAINTAIN 0.95 MACH TO CRUISE ALTITUDE.

● TIME FROM BRAKE RELEASE TO INITIAL CLIMB SPEED IS 0.5 MINUTES.

DATE: 1 MARCH 1977
DATA BASIS: **ESTIMATED**

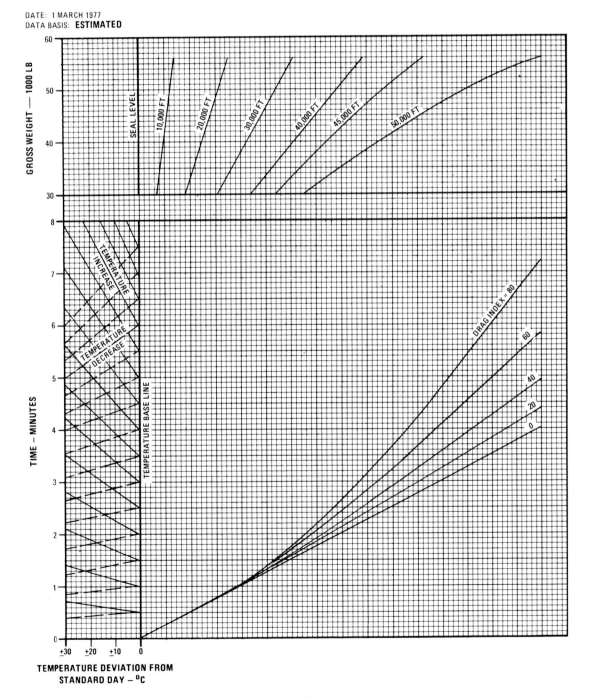

As of January 1, 1978, there are no longer any TF-15s in the USAF inventory. Engineering Change Proposal (ECP) 975 will redesignate the *Eagle* to readily differentiate the mission capabilities. The PEP-2000 program (ECP 450) which added 2,000 pounds of internal fuel and the hardware for adding the conformal tanks (FAST Packs) will be added and the corresponding designations will be as follows on the next page.

F-15 SERIES — SERIAL NUMBER CONVERSION CHART — ADPLS TABLE NO. 06

PAGE 1 — 15 MARCH 1976

Detail Spec.: TF-15A CP76301A328A020 ADDENDUM "A"; F-15A CP76301A328A020 — Contract Number: F33657-70-C-0300

DETAIL SPEC.	CONTRACT NUMBER	BLOCK NO. QTY ( )	MCAIR AIRCRAFT NUMBER	F-15A AIR FORCE SERIAL NUMBERS	CUM AIRCRAFT	TF-15A AIR FORCE SERIAL NUMBERS	CUM AIRCRAFT
				J.O. 660	FY 1970	J.O. 661	
		BLOCK 1	1	71-280	1		
		QTY (2)	2	71-281	2		
		TOTAL BLOCK 1			(2)		
		BLOCK 2	3	71-282	3		
		QTY (3)	4	71-283	4		
			5	71-284	5		
		TOTAL BLOCK 2			(3)		
		BLOCK 3	6	71-285	6		
		QTY (3)	7	71-286	7		
			8			71-290	1
		TOTAL BLOCK 3			(2)		(1)
		BLOCK 4	9	71-287	8		
		QTY (4)	10	71-288	9		
			11	71-289	10		
			12			71-291	2
		TOTAL BLOCK 4			(3)		(1)
				J.O. 663	FY 1972		
		BLOCK 5	13	72-113	11		
		QTY (4)	14	72-114	12		
			15	72-115	13		
			16	72-116	14		
		TOTAL BLOCK 5			(4)		
		BLOCK 6	17	72-117	15		
		QTY (4)	18	72-118	16		
			19	72-119	17		
			20	72-120	18		
		TOTAL BLOCK 6			(4)		
				J.O. 664 FY 1973		J.O. 666 FY 1973	
			21			73-108	3
			22			73-109	4
			23	73-085	19		
		BLOCK 7	24	73-086	20		
		QTY (8)	25			73-110	5
			26	73-087	21		
			27	73-088	22		
			28	73-089	23		
		TOTAL BLOCK 7			(5)		(3)
			29			73-111	6
		BLOCK 8	30	73-090	24		
		QTY (10)	31	73-091	25		
		BLOCK 8 CONTINUED ON NEXT PAGE					

GP76-6022-2

F-15 SERIES — SERIAL NUMBER CONVERSION CHART — ADPLS TABLE NO. 06

PAGE 2 — 15 MARCH 1976

Detail Spec.: TF-15A CP76301A328A020 ADDENDUM "A"; F-15A CP76301A328A020 — Contract Number: F33657-70-C-0300

DETAIL SPEC.	CONTRACT NUMBER	BLOCK NO. QTY ( )	MCAIR AIRCRAFT NUMBER	F-15A AIR FORCE SERIAL NUMBERS	CUM AIRCRAFT	TF-15A AIR FORCE SERIAL NUMBERS	CUM AIRCRAFT
				J.O. 664 FY 1973		J.O. 666 FY 1973	
			32			73-112	7
			33	73-092	26		
		BLOCK 8	34	73-093	27		
		QTY (10)	35	73-094	28		
			36	73-095	29		
			37	73-096	30		
			38	73-097	31		
		TOTAL BLOCK 8			(8)		(2)
			39			73-113	8
			40	73-098	32		
			41			73-114	9
			42	73-099	33		
		BLOCK 9	43	73-100	34		
		QTY (12)	44	73-101	35		
			45	73-102	36		
			46	73-103	37		
			47	73-104	38		
			48	73-105	39		
			49	73-106	40		
			50	73-107	41		
		TOTAL BLOCK 9			(10)		(2)
				J.O. 668 FY 1974		J.O. 669 FY 1974	
			51	74-081	42		
			52			74-137	10
			53	74-082	43		
			54			74-138	11
			55	74-083	44		
			56	74-084	45		
		BLOCK 10	57	74-085	46		
		QTY (15)	58	74-086	47		
			59	74-087	48		
			60	74-088	49		
			61	74-089	50		
			62	74-090	51		
			63	74-091	52		
			64	74-092	53		
			65	74-093	54		
		TOTAL BLOCK 10			(13)		(2)
			66			74-139	12
		BLOCK 11	67	74-094	55		
		QTY (20)	68	74-095	56		
		BLOCK 11 CONTINUED ON NEXT PAGE					

GP76-6022-3

F-15 SERIES — SERIAL NUMBER CONVERSION CHART — ADPLS TABLE NO. 06

PAGE 3 — 09 APRIL 1976

Detail Spec.: TF-15A CP76301A328A020 ADDENDUM "A"; F-15A CP76301A328A020 — Contract Number: F33657-70-C-0300

DETAIL SPEC.	CONTRACT NUMBER	BLOCK NO. QTY ( )	MCAIR AIRCRAFT NUMBER	F-15A AIR FORCE SERIAL NUMBERS	CUM AIRCRAFT	TF-15A AIR FORCE SERIAL NUMBERS	CUM AIRCRAFT
				J.O. 668 FY 1974		J.O. 669 FY 1974	
			69			74-140	13
			70	74-096	57		
			71	74-097	58		
			72	74-098	59		
			73	74-099	60		
			74	74-100	61		
			75	74-101	62		
		BLOCK 11	76	74-102	63		
		QTY (20)	77	74-103	64		
			78	74-104	65		
			79	74-105	66		
			80	74-106	67		
			81	74-107	68		
			82	74-108	69		
			83	74-109	70		
			84	74-110	71		
			85	74-111	72		
		TOTAL BLOCK 11			(18)		(2)
			86			74-141	14
			87	74-112	73		
			88	74-113	74		
			89	74-114	75		
			90			74-142	15
			91	74-115	76		
			92	74-116	77		
			93	74-117	78		
			94	74-118	79		
			95	74-119	80		
			96	74-120	81		
		BLOCK 12	97	74-121	82		
		QTY (27)	98	74-122	83		
			99	74-123	84		
			100	74-124	85		
			101	74-125	86		
			102	74-126	87		
			103	74-127	88		
			104	74-128	89		
			105	74-129	90		
			106	74-130	91		
			107	74-131	92		
			108	74-132	93		
			109	74-133	94		
			110	74-134	95		
			111	74-135	96		
			112	74-136	97		
		TOTAL BLOCK 12			(25)		(2)

GP76-6022-4

F-15 SERIES — SERIAL NUMBER CONVERSION CHART — ADPLS TABLE NO. 06

PAGE 4 — 09 APRIL 1976

Detail Spec.: TF-15A CP76301A328A020 ADDENDUM "A"; F-15A CP76301A328A020 — Contract Number: F33657-70-C-0300

DETAIL SPEC.	CONTRACT NUMBER	BLOCK NO. QTY ( )	MCAIR AIRCRAFT NUMBER	F-15A AIR FORCE SERIAL NUMBERS	CUM AIRCRAFT	TF-15A AIR FORCE SERIAL NUMBERS	CUM AIRCRAFT
				J.O. 677 FY 1975		J.O. 678 FY 1975	
			113	75-0018	98		
			114			75-0080	16
			115	75-0019	99		
			116	75-0020	100		
			117	75-0021	101		
			118	75-0022	102		
			119	75-0023	103		
			120			75-0081	17
			121	75-0024	104		
			122	75-0025	105		
			123	75-0026	106		
			124	75-0027	107		
			125	75-0028	108		
			126	75-0029	109		
			127			75-0082	18
			128	75-0030	110		
			129	75-0031	111		
		BLOCK 13	130	75-0032	112		
		QTY (36)	131	75-0033	113		
			132	75-0034	114		
			133	75-0035	115		
			134	75-0036	116		
			135			75-0083	19
			136	75-0037	117		
			137	75-0038	118		
			138	75-0039	119		
			139	75-0040	120		
			140	75-0041	121		
			141	75-0042	122		
			142	75-0043	123		
			143			75-0084	20
			144	75-0044	124		
			145	75-0045	125		
			146	75-0046	126		
			147	75-0047	127		
			148	75-0048	128		
		TOTAL BLOCK 13			(31)		(5)

GP76-6022-5